CLASSIC CRAFTS

CLASSIC CRAFTS
A PRACTICAL COMPENDIUM OF
TRADITIONAL SKILLS

PHOTOGRAPHY BY JACQUI HURST

GENERAL EDITOR MARTINA MARGETTS

SIMON AND SCHUSTER

NEW YORK LONDON TORONTO SYDNEY TOKYO

I would like to thank the craftspeople who kindly allowed me to
photograph their work; Martina Margetts and the staff at Conran Octopus,
in particular, Prue Bucknall, Mary Evans, Cortina Butler,
Jane Harcus and Abigail Ahern; Nester MacDonald and Janet Henderson
for their help and encouragement; and David Robertson
for his invaluable support.

JACQUI HURST

Simon and Schuster
Simon & Schuster Building
Rockefeller Center
1230 Avenue of the Americas
New York, New York 10020

First published in 1989 in Great Britain by
Conran Octopus Limited
37 Shelton Street
London WC2H 9HN

Art Director Mary Evans

Art Editor Prue Bucknall

Project Editor Cortina Butler

Editor Jane Harcus

Copy Editors Eleanor Van Zandt and
Michelle Clark

Production Graham Darlow

Illustrators Nick Asher, Lucy Su and
Kejkanoek Uawithya

Contributors Anne Boston, David Briers, Frances Bugg,
Margot Coatts, Peter Dormer, Lucinda Gane,
Rosemary Hill, Jacqui Hurst, Pamela Johnson and
Martina Margetts

Printed and bound in Italy

1 3 5 7 9 10 8 6 4 2

Library of Congress Cataloging in Publication Data

Classic crafts : a practical compendium of traditional skills /
photography by Jacqui Hurst.
p. cm.
Includes index.
ISBN 0-671-68739-5
1. Handicraft. I. Hurst, Jacqui. II Simon and Schuster, inc.
TT157. C514 1990
745—dc20 89-10107
CIP

KITCHEN CRAFTS

GOAT CHEESE 110
FESTIVAL BREAD 116
COOKIE MAKING 122
SMOKING FISH 124
CHOCOLATE MAKING 128
PRESERVES 132
CIDER MAKING 140
BASKETRY 144
DRIED FLOWERS 150
CANDLE MAKING 158

DECORATIVE CRAFTS

164 STICK DRESSING
170 GILDING
176 CARVED BIRDS
184 TOY MAKING
190 LEATHERWORK
196 SPONGEWARE
202 STENCILED TILES
206 STAINED GLASS
214 JEWELRY

INDEX 220
ACKNOWLEDGMENTS 223

INTRODUCTION

A S WE APPROACH THE YEAR 2000, mankind is experiencing a heightened awareness of the vulnerability of our planet. There is an urgent need to preserve the balance of nature on which survival depends. Perhaps this underlies the widespread interest in the creative activities which define and determine our quality of life. Man's search for originality and innovation in all things is now tempered by an appreciation of continuing traditions.

The crafts – utilitarian or contemplative objects made by hand – have received renewed attention in the past two decades. They are people's most direct, tangible link with their surroundings. Once the tools of everyday life, they are now more a medium for the appreciation of skills, beauty and, obliquely, a commentary on life. If we can appre-

ciate the crafts, in all their astonishing variety, from conventional works of fine craftsmanship to the most extreme expressions of the creative avant-garde, we have a strong and enduring link with societies of the past and the present.

The crafts revival in the West of the past two decades has been spearheaded by an avant-garde élite, nurtured by art schools and arts organizations, which felt free to manipulate the traditions of craft techniques, materials, and styles to produce innovative work in all media. Ceramics, textiles, jewelry, furniture and, more recently, craft disciplines such as glass, bookworks, and basketry have all been redefined. Purposes and meanings, colors, scale, form, value, approaches to construction, have all been challenged and re-presented. A clay teapot need no longer pour, a book

nomic, and cultural development.

The boom in world travel, in media, and communications has shrunk our world, providing much common ground for appreciating human achievement. But perhaps what this global village especially values are the inherent differences in societies. This is a starting-point for the crafts, where the hand and mind of the maker produces works of unmistakable individuality, even where the conventions of an object are strongly rooted. In craftwork, the resolution into a single object from particular choices of materials, colors, shapes, and techniques is a constant source of wonder and delight to enthusiastic observers.

The crafts in this book introduce the reader to the quality and individuality within a tradition of a range of con-temporary crafts. The craftspeople, leaders in their field, span decades of experience (the oldest is 85) and attest to the fascinating evolution of craft traditions. Some of the crafts are esoteric, some well known, some rely on the quality of raw materials and workmanship for their appeal, others on individual pattern-making in the design and surface decoration. Yet all the work is domestic in scale and echoes the dictum of that most famous nineteenth-century crafts pioneer, William Morris: "Have nothing in your home that you do not know to be useful and believe to be beautiful."

In highlighting the practicalities of creating crafts by hand, by giving specific instructions on how to make craft objects, the book offers a telling insight into the patient workmanship and stead-fast vision of leading craftspeople. But these insights are not exclusive: readers should be inspired, not daunted, by the range of work shown and encouraged to use the projects as starting points to practice the handling of materials and tools, methods, and techniques and then to evolve their own ideas in the crafts which most interest them.

This book provides a rare opportunity to have explanations of so many different living craft traditions gathered together. It conveys the fascinating and enduring interrelationship between the crafts – pottery and breadmaking, basketry and weaving, patchwork, and stained glass – and reveals the variety of human experience possible through the medium of handwork.

MARTINA MARGETTS

HAND BLOCK PRINTING

PATTERN MAKING
*Hand-carved blocks and richly-colored dyes
are used to create intricate and unusual
printed fabrics.*

HAND BLOCK PRINTING FIRST appeared in the East, where textile makers initially painted their designs onto fabric, then introduced small printing blocks which made it possible to repeat certain motifs more quickly. Eventually they made blocks to contain the entire pattern. These Eastern printed textiles, imported into Europe in quantity from the seventeenth century, were known as "chintz." Often their patterns were created by combining several techniques, including resist printing (using wax), mordant dyeing (a treatment in which the fabric is printed with mineral salts so that it will accept certain dyes), and discharge dyeing (in which bleaches wash the dye out, leaving a white pattern).

In England and France block printing expertise developed in competition with Eastern imports and rose to its height in the period 1750–1850. The industry made use of designers and a variety of tradesmen: block makers to transfer designs to multiple blocks and work out the repeats; cloth buyers to acquire suitable fabrics; and printers and their assistants to fix the dyes and clean and dry the fabrics. By the mid nineteenth century, however, roller printing began to overtake block printing, and hand skills were on the decline. Simultaneously, there was feverish experimentation with dyes and in 1856 chemical colors were discovered. Traditional dyeing methods were swept aside and "natural" dyestuffs were almost totally abandoned.

In the latter part of the nineteenth century William Morris, with his firm Morris and Co. of London, in reaction to the mechanization of the textile industries, began to design textiles and print them by hand, using blocks and, wherever possible, natural dyestuffs. By the 1920s several craftsmen, influenced by the work of Morris, had started block-printing workshops of their own.

The modern block printer and dyer needs to accommodate all the traditional factory processes in a single workshop. For this professional printer, the first requirement is a solid table, measuring about 1 x 2 yds (1 x 2 m), with the top at approximately waist height. Of equal importance are: a good supply of untreated running water; deep, low-set porcelain sinks, one with a wringer attached; and drainage gullies, above which wet lengths of cloth are left to dry. An old washing machine is necessary and a cast-iron stove cooks the dyes

DRYING CLOTH
*Pieces of cloth dyed using the traditional resist
method are dried in the fresh air.*

and provides hot water. A concrete trough for dip-dyeing and clean areas for planning, cutting, and sewing are also useful facilities.

The blocks themselves are cut from thick linoleum (mid-brown in color and of fine consistency), glued, under pressure, to strips of seasoned hardwood or 5-ply board using all-purpose adhesive. Many printers prefer the blocks to be a manageable hand-size – that is, about 10 in (25 cm) long by 2 in (5 cm) wide. The linoleum is cut with any blade, gouge, or scriber capable of making the chosen shape, mark, or texture; homemade tools are often the best. Blocks must be tested frequently during cutting, for it is the subtlety of the relationships between them, and the colors on them, that is the clever part of the pattern-making process. Color is a

personal matter – there are no rules – but the combination of a strong color for the back print and a lighter one on top is often successful. The choice of dyes is more a matter of finance: a single "family" of dyestuffs, including fixing agents, can be a very heavy outlay; in addition, it takes a long time to learn to use one system well. Experience shows that, currently, fiber-reactive dyes are a reliable choice for the small operator.

Fabric printers like to collect a number of short lengths of plain unbleached muslin cottons, and other silks, and linens, or cloth with a woven stripe or spot, on which to work. The fabric to be

FLOUR PASTE PATTERNS
*Fabric has been painted with a mixture of
flour and water and then hung up to dry.*

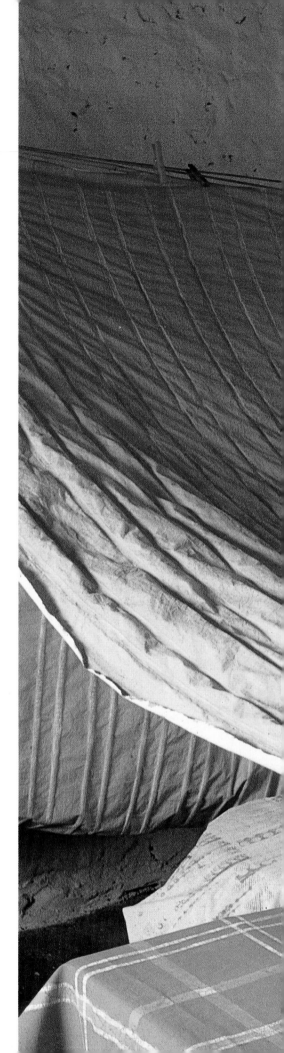

TEXTILE CRAFTS

HAND BLOCK PRINTING □ QUILTING

PATCHWORK □ APPLIQUÉ □ SMOCKING

DYEING AND KNITTING □ TASSELS AND BRAIDS

IKAT WEAVING □ RAG RUGS

PREPARATION AND PRINTING

A pattern is cut into the linoleum (right), the dyepad is brushed evenly with dye and, finally, a print can be taken.

A CORNER OF THE WORK AREA

Every part of this room has been adapted to cater for the printer's needs.

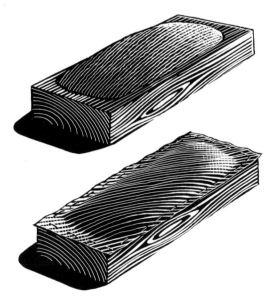

MAKING A DYEPAD

Cover a block of wood with a pad of blanket. Protect the pad with a waterproof layer and staple or nail a piece of blanket over it.

<u>THE NECK SCARF</u>
*Simple hand-stitched garments complement
the fine patterning of block prints.*

printed must first be boiled, washed, rinsed, dried, and ironed very carefully to ensure that it is "square." One day should be allowed for this. On the same day, mix up the dyes, following the manufacturer's instructions. Put the backing cloth on the print table. To do this, paint the surface of an old table with table gum. When it is tacky, lay a piece of clean, ironed cotton cloth on it. Rule pencil lines along its length, perfectly parallel, to act as guides for the selvages of the fabric to be printed.

Place the fabric to be printed on the table (it can be pinned to the backing cloth – although an experienced printer will not need to pin). Rule a soft pencil line down the fabric's center; the design is printed outward from this line in bands running from top to bottom.

On the second day the printing can begin. The following equipment is required: two blocks, a dyepad (a padded, fabric-covered board, like a palette), two paintbrushes, rubber gloves and a protective apron.

First, place a bowl of dye, the brushes, and the dyepad in a convenient position, away from the print table. Brush the dye onto the pad, pick the dye up with the first block, and apply it to the cloth along the center. The pattern edge forms its own guideline. When the length is completed, leave it to dry for anything from one to three hours, depending on the room temperature and the absorbency of the fabric. Now, overprint the fabric with the next block in a second color.

Fix the dye, following the manufacturer's instructions, and rinse the cloth thoroughly. Then put it through a

hot soapy wash in a washing machine, rinse it again and dry it in the open air. Iron the fabric well.

An effective way to show off a hand-block-printed design is to wear it as a shawl around the shoulders or as a neck scarf. To make a shawl, cut an exact square, using the guidelines already drawn on the print table; to make two triangular neck scarves, cut this in half again diagonally. Using a warm iron, press under a hem of ⅜ in (1 cm), mitring the corners neatly and cutting off the points. Take the shawl or neck scarf to a good light, and, with the point of a needle, roll the raw edge under, right into the crease of the hem, and secure it with a very neat slipstitch; use thread of the same fiber as the cloth but a shade darker in color. Finally, steam-press the edges lightly.

QUILTING

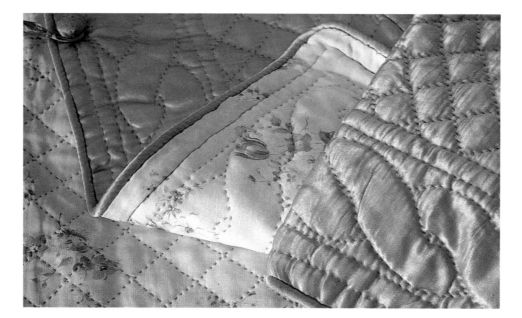

FINE, TRADITIONAL STITCHING
*Exquisite quilting from the North of England
looks rich, and its beauty is as appealing
today as ever.*

QUILTING IS A METHOD OF STITCH-ing layers of fabric together to form a strong, warm, and decorative material. Thought to be one of the oldest types of needlework, it has been used over the years for vests, petticoats, wedding gowns, and other elaborate clothing, and even for armor. In the home, bed-covers, pillows, and, more recently, decorative wall-hangings have all employed the same technique to wonderful effect. Some contemporary quilt-makers have raised their hangings and screens to the level of fine art.

In the seventeenth and eighteenth centuries, garments decorated with quilting were the height of fashion. The mid-eighteenth century, however, saw the advent of printed fabrics, and patch-work garments became popular as a quicker, less expensive alternative. A

later development was the introduction of mass-produced quilted fabric which, to some extent, took over from hand quilting. Nevertheless, traditional hand quilting survived, and the items produced were a source of great pride and an important part of daily life in many country homes.

Hand quilting stitches are charact-eristically small and even, involving a high degree of skill and a keen eye. Plain, wholecloth quilts rely on a com-bination of fabric, stitching, and pattern for their effect. The play of light on the delicately sculptured surface of the finished article is all-important.

The fabric chosen for quilting needs to reflect the light, but a high gloss is not always necessary. Plain, closely-woven, natural materials, such as silk or good-quality cotton, are ideal. The batting has

to be of good quality, as does the thread used, and the best results come from an organized approach.

A complete hand-made quilt is a huge undertaking, involving hundreds of hours of painstaking work. Impressive results can, however, be produced on a smaller scale, and traditional patterns can be adapted to create lovely pieces.

The round, quilted silk pillow featured (right), employs traditional patterns from the North of England. The top of the pillow has a central rose motif with a 4 in (10 cm) cable border with diamond infill, the side strip and base are decorated with a simple basket pattern, and two rows of silk cording finish off the design.

You will need some patience to com-plete this project, but the results are well worth the effort.

MARKING THE FABRIC
*Patterns are transferred to the fabric using a
white china marker.*

SETTING UP THE FRAME
*The layers of fabric are sewn onto the
webbing at the top of the quilting frame.*

To make a round pillow that measures 22 in (56 cm) in diameter the following materials are needed: 1½ yds (1.4 m) of 45 in (115 cm) wide pure satin silk in cream; the same of fine, white linen, and the same of medium-loft polyester batting; a pillow pad for stuffing the pillow; two 100 yd (100 m) spools of quilting, or silk, thread of the best quality in a matching cream color; 2½ yds (2.3 m) of filler cord; and tracing paper. Also needed are the following items of equipment: a wooden quilting frame; trestles or chairs to support the frame; cotton tape; fine quilting needles; a thimble; two pairs of scissors, one large, one small; dressmaker's pins; a tape measure; a white china marker or chinagraph pencil; quilting stencils or patterns made from card for the central rose motif, the cable border, the

diamond, and basket patterns; a dressmaker's marking wheel; a blunt needle or a cobbler's awl; and a leathercloth, or an equivalent surface, that you can stick a needle into without damage, for "marking out" on.

Ideally, the fabric being quilted should be set in a traditional quilting frame, as the material is less likely to pull. It keeps clean this way, and it can be left, set up ready to work on at any time. The width of the fabric given will provide the front and back of the pillow plus a side strip measuring 63 x 4 in (160 x 10 cm). Sew the silk, batting, and linen together at the edges, keeping them flat, silk uppermost, right side up, batting sandwiched in the middle, and white linen beneath.

The pattern is marked on the silk before the layers of fabric are put in the

frame. The way it is marked is a matter of personal taste, but a wide variety of markers is available. Originally white blackboard chalk would have been used to draw around templates, drinking glasses, saucers, fingers, and other suitable items for making patterns. In this instance, however, the use of a white china marker is recommended. If the marker is used lightly it can be rubbed off with a towel or a dry sponge when the quilting has been completed.

Templates, available as individual patterns, from books or quilters' shops, can be traced onto tracing paper and then transferred to the top fabric by placing the greaseproof paper on the fabric and pricking through the paper and into the fabric with a blunt needle or better still, an awl. With this method, the basic outline is usually pricked on

WORKING WITH THE FRAME
*Once the frame has been set up, quilting can
proceed at leisure.*

QUILTING THE PILLOW
*Work first around the edges of the design
using tiny, even running stitches.*

and the fine details of the pattern are filled in by hand. Alternatively, plastic stencils can be placed directly on the fabric and then drawn around.

Once the pattern for the top, base, and side strip of the pillow is marked, set all three layers into the frame by first pinning or basting the fabric to the webbing at the top and bottom of the frame. Carefully roll the material onto the back rail, leaving one arm's length on which to work. Roll it up as the work proceeds. Tape the sides of the fabric to the sides of the frame to keep the work even, pinning it in place every 2 in (5 cm).

Three or more stitches can be worked and kept on the needle at one time, before pulling the thread through, and both hands should be free to sew. Wear a thimble on the middle finger of the upper hand, and use the other hand underneath the work to guide the needle back through. Always work in a good natural light, and aim to generate a natural rocking rhythm, as this will contribute toward fine, even sewing.

First, quilt around the perimeter of each 22 in (56 cm) diameter circle, then quilt the pattern from front to back and right to left, taking care to keep the silk clean. To progress evenly across the pillow it may be necessary to have more than one needle in use. Approach the side strip in the same way. Start and finish off neatly. Any mistakes should be removed from the back, as this will reduce the possibility of snagging the silk. If you should prick your finger and a drop of blood falls on the silk, do not panic – reliable sources say that it can be removed with some spittle on a small piece of batting. Traditionally, a record

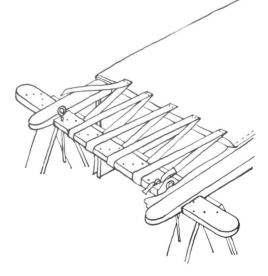

A QUILTING FRAME
*The fabric is securely stitched and taped onto
the edges of the frame.*

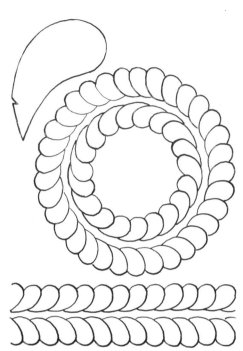

THE TEAR SHAPE
This useful pattern can be adapted for round or square designs.

CONTINUITY AND PATTERNING
When stitching, it is important to follow the natural lines of the pattern wherever possible.

is kept of the time spent quilting by marking off the hours on the frame itself. When each piece is finished, cut it from the frame, leaving a border.

To make up the pillow, first prepare a length of cording. Cut bias strips from the remaining silk, sew them together, and then wrap the long strip around the cording. Pin the cording to the right side of the top and bottom pieces, so that the raw edges are together and the covered cord lies just inside the seam-line. Baste it in place. Sew the ends of the side strip together to form a ring. Pin one long edge to the top piece, right sides together. Baste the seam, and then sew it together. Attach the bottom piece to the side strip in the same way, leaving a space for filling the pillow with the pad. Insert the pillow pad and slipstitch the edges together.

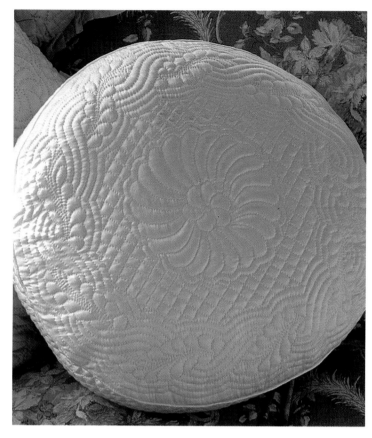

THE QUILTED PILLOW
The finished pillow above, and traditional basket pattern top right.

THE BORDER AND ROSE MOTIF
There are many variations of this popular cable border and rose pattern.

PATCHWORK

<u>INTERLOCKING PATCHES OF FABRIC</u>
*Fabric pieces are joined by tiny whipstitches
to form an intricate design – the back is
almost as perfect as the front.*

PATCHWORK HAS A LONG AND DIS-tinguished history. From earliest times, when woven materials and animal skins were in short supply, there must have been an urgent need to mend with patches, to make new garments or furnishings incorporating usable parts of articles that were worn or damaged, or simply to join left-over scraps of material to make larger pieces of fabric.

The current upsurge of interest in patchwork tends to focus on its relatively recent history in North America and Europe. On both sides of the Atlantic it served as a way by which people of slender means could furnish themselves with patchwork quilts and other useful household articles, and the more rich and leisured could engage in a pleasurable and rewarding occupation. The women's movement has seized on patch-work quilts as examples of the abundant creativity of women denied by social circumstances the opportunity for self-expression in the more prominent branches of the visual arts; and it is true that women with little or no artistic background produced an astonishing number of rich, subtle, and varied textiles. Examples of their work can be found in textile collections in many major museums.

There are several different styles and methods of making patchwork. The most familiar is pieced or mosaic patchwork, in which the entire surface is made up of small interlocking units of fabric which may be different in shape – or identical – provided they fit together like the pieces of a jig-saw puzzle. Log cabin is another well-known patchwork pattern. It also consists of repeating blocks, but they are sewn to a backing fabric and made up into a series of square frames, radiating outward from a central square. The arrangement of colors within the frames, and the relationship between juxtaposed blocks, produces a wide range of effects. Appliqué patchwork, in which motifs are slip-stitched to a backing fabric, produces figurative and abstract designs with equal ease. Many of the basic patchwork techniques are readily modified for machine-sewing. The log cabin pattern, where seams are straight and regular, is the most obvious example.

Two distinct methods of sewing pieced patchwork together have evolved over the centuries. In the farming communities of North America, where time was relatively scarce, patches were joined with ordinary seams using a

need not open, a chair can be uncomfortable but sculptural, a necklace so big and bizarre it suggests performance art, a textile "an environmental statement in fiber." Significantly, the best of such work owes its convincing virtuosity to the thoroughness with which its makers have first learned and then re-interpreted crafts' cultural and technical traditions. In the flowering of a crafts avant-garde, the diverse traditions of craft have been the fertile soil.

There are several reasons why the last two decades have witnessed a ferment in the crafts. The 1960s saw a marked increase in the West of craft courses in art schools, notably in ceramics, textiles, and jewelry. The status of the crafts was raised, since students studied alongside painters and sculptors, filmmakers and industrial designers. The decline of the traditional craft apprenticeship system aligned craftspeople more closely with their peer group in other art forms. This more sophisticated craft education, with its emphasis on design, broadened the career paths of the greatly increased number of craft graduates. Links, which had developed during the twentieth century, could be cemented with the worlds of interior, industrial, theater and product design, with architecture, fashion, and performance art. Many graduates became the teachers of the next generation. By the end of the 1970s, the broader base of professionalism in the crafts was established; the hippie, amateurish connotations of crafts in the 1960s had been banished.

While the world of the craft practitioner changed, so did that of the consumer. Increased wealth and leisure time has given many more people the opportunity either to take up a craft or to pursue their enthusiasms as craft collectors, exhibition goers, magazine readers, and bespoke homemakers. The greater sophistication of mass-produced goods has heightened people's discrimination of the design and quality of workmanship in objects. The crafts have come into their own as offering the best-made or the most individualistic solutions to many kinds of everyday object. Because of their comparative rarity, expense, and individual design, craftworks have become, as it were, the loss-leaders of our consumer society. Museums worldwide collect contemporary decorative and applied arts to present the best and most unusual of what is made now. The crafts can be seen as visual touchstones of social, eco-

CONTENTS

INTRODUCTION 8

TEXTILE CRAFTS
HAND BLOCK PRINTING 14
QUILTING 20
PATCHWORK 26
APPLIQUÉ 32
SMOCKING 38
DYEING AND KNITTING 44
TASSELS AND BRAIDS 54
IKAT WEAVING 60
RAG RUGS 66

PAPER CRAFTS
74 PAPERMAKING
78 PAPERMARBLING
84 CALLIGRAPHY
88 WOOD ENGRAVING
92 LETTERPRESS PRINTING
98 BOOKBINDING
102 PAPIER MÂCHÉ

DESIGNING A PILLOW
*Draw design ideas onto graph paper (left)
and experiment with colors and shapes.*

PATCHWORK TEMPLATES

*Household objects can be traced for
alternative shapes, or buy templates.*

simple running stitch. For the work
shown here, the more accurate, stronger
method is used to produce highly
defined units. The fabric shapes are
basted to paper templates and joined
with tiny whipstitches.

Anyone who does household sewing
or dressmaking will have most of the
equipment needed for sewing patchwork; cutting-out scissors, needlework
scissors with sharp points for snipping
threads, fine sewing needles, thread (for
basting and sewing) and, of course, the
fabric itself. Cotton fabrics should be
washed in advance to check for color-
fastness and shrinkage. If old fabrics are

PINNING AND CUTTING

*Cut out all the paper shapes for each color
and pin them onto the fabric.*

<u>ASSEMBLING THE PIECES</u>
*Turn under fabric margins and roughly baste
them in place.*

used, they should be subjected to vigorous pulling and stretching to make sure they are strong enough. The fabrics in a piece of patchwork should all be of approximately the same weight and preferably of the same fiber content, if the work is to be washed. Thread color should be chosen to blend as nearly as possible with the fabrics.

For designing patterns and making templates, the following equipment is required: graph paper, a steel ruler to provide a firm cutting edge, a cutting board, a craft knife, stiff cardboard, paper-cutting scissors, and paper.

The three-color pillow shown completed overleaf, measures 20 in (50 cm) square and requires ¼ yd (20 cm) each of the rust and yellow fabrics and 1 yd (90 cm) of turquoise fabric, which is also used for the back of the pillow.

Begin by drawing the patchwork block design to scale onto graph paper following the illustration (right). The finished block is 4 in (10 cm) square. Each small square in the illustration corresponds to 1 in (2.5 cm) square, so it is easy to draw it up to scale. This design could be divided in various ways but it works successfully with the yellow star shape made up of a central square and four triangles. Two rust squares, four rust parallelograms, and four turquoise triangles complete the basic block – six shapes in all. A total of 13 patchwork blocks are needed for this pillow. In addition, 12 squares of plain turquoise fabric, cut to the same size as the finished patchwork block, are used to complete the design.

Each shape must then be accurately transferred onto cardboard (which must

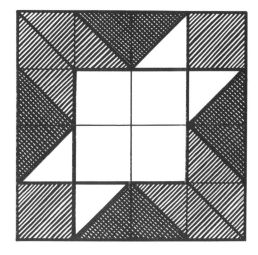

<u>THE PATCHWORK BLOCK</u>
*Draw this pattern to scale on graph paper:
1 square of the pattern equals 1 in (2.5 cm)
square. A total of 13 assembled blocks are
needed for the pillow.*

29

MAKING UP THE PILLOW
*Sew all the patchwork blocks before attaching
the turquoise squares.*

THE COMPLETED PILLOW
*As well as this pillow, patchwork can be used
to make quilts and wall-hangings.*

be stiff enough to stand wear) and cut out using the craft knife and steel rule. The more accurate the cardboard templates are, the less adjustment there will have to be later on; it is a good idea to check the templates against each other for the best fit possible. It is also useful to indicate on each template the direction in which the lengthwise grain of the fabric should run (a bias-cut piece will distort easily and cause unsightly puckering), and to write on each template the number of paper templates required.

Place the cardboard templates on the paper, draw around them and cut out the shapes. If six sheets of paper are firmly held together with tape or paper-clips, six templates can be cut at a time, but they should always be checked against the cardboard template.

Arrange the paper templates along the straight grain of the fabric, and pin them in place, allowing a margin of not less than ¼ in (5 mm) on all edges. Cut out the shapes, fold over the fabric margins and baste them in place. When all the pieces have been made up, the assembling can begin. Place two pieces together with right sides facing and with the edges to be joined aligned precisely. Picking up as few threads as possible with the needle, work tiny whipstitches over both edges, so that a diagonal stitch shows on the wrong side, and a small straight stitch is barely visible on the right side. The stitches should be small and regular and the thread fastened securely at both ends. Pieces of the same color are usually joined first. In this case the yellow star is assembled and the rust parallelograms joined in pairs. The rust shapes and turquoise triangles are then attached to the yellow star to make a complete patchwork block.

When the composite blocks are finished, join these to the plain turquoise squares. Remove the basting threads, but not the paper templates, and press the work on the right side, with a press cloth, then remove the paper. Baste along the edges of the finished square, tucking in loose corners or "flags," and holding the seam allowance in place. Any excessively long or intrusive flags should be trimmed – particularly if they are likely to show through on the right side. It is a good idea to back the patchwork, for strength and neatness, with unbleached muslin. The patchwork could either be hand-appliquéd or basted and machine-stitched to the backing fabric. The pillow cover can then be made up in the usual way.

APPLIQUÉ

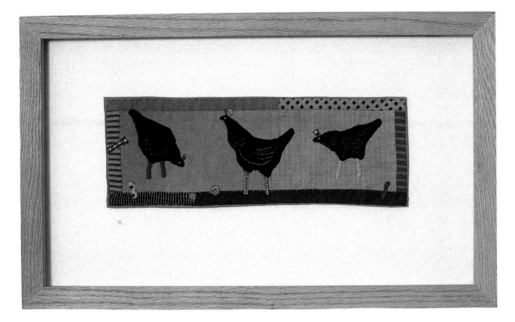

"THREE HENS"
*To create the right balance the artist must
make a careful choice from a large collection
of fabrics.*

THE WORD "APPLIQUÉ" COMES from the French verb meaning "to apply," and refers to the technique of fixing shaped pieces of cloth to a background fabric. Appliqué has been used for centuries in many cultures, including those of ancient Egypt, India, and medieval and Renaissance Europe. It is very simple, but the effect can be striking with strong shapes on a contrasting ground. The skill lies in choosing the fabrics and in cutting and placing the images; an eye for color and pattern is the key to this craft. The sewing is done with a simple slipstitch, but more elaborate embroidery stitches can be used to embellish the work.

Appliqué is often used in conjunction with the related techniques of patchwork and quilting; embroiderers also use appliqué for a variety of effects. Its main use, traditionally, has been for domestic furnishings, such as quilts, wall-hangings, and pillows, but it can be used to decorate clothing. The technique also lends itself to picture-making, in which case composition and balance, as well as color, are important.

Building up a picture begins intuitively by selecting suitable fabrics. This is a search for complementary fabrics: colors, patterns, and textures that will best convey the image in the artist's mind – or even suggest new images. When making a small or medium-sized picture, it is advisable to use solid-colored fabrics or those with an appropriately sized pattern, such as small dots or checks. Warm, earthy tones make a pleasing background.

Having achieved a satisfactory background, the artist will build up the com-position, starting with the central image. Each cut-out element is pinned to the ground. The artist may then leave the work and return to it with fresh eyes to see if the composition is right. At this stage, elements can be added or taken away. Colors can be changed or texture and pattern added. The fabric itself will suggest ideas, and, having no rigid design, the artist can change the composition at any stage. More pattern or color can be added later by stitching over the appliquéd image. Often, the most effective pictures are produced by keeping the composition simple. When the composition seems right, the pieces are stitched in place, starting with the main image. This can be done by using the needle to turn the edge, then working a simple slipstitch.

When the picture is complete, it is

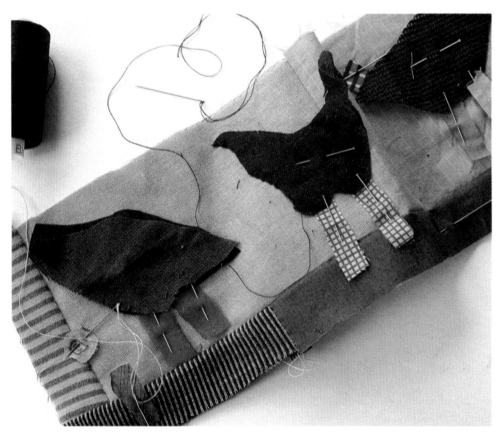

SELECTING AND SHAPING
Always try to focus the viewer's eye on the central images.

mounted on plain cloth to provide extra thickness. The artist can then quilt large areas of the plain background, using a running stitch, to create additional texture. The quilting should suggest a "drawn" line.

The "Three Hens" picture (see previous page) uses the recurring image of a hen to create a pleasing and cohesive composition, but other themes such as ducks, kites, hot-air balloons, and flowers could be used to equal effect. It is the figurative simplicity of the image that is important.

The materials required for the "Three Hens" picture are: two pieces of solid-colored fabric for the background, large enough to create a "canvas" measuring about 4 x 12 in (10 x 30 cm) when sewn together; a selection of patterned and solid-colored fabrics (preferably

SEWING THE PICTURE
*Stitching will alter the size of each element –
stand back to check the balance.*

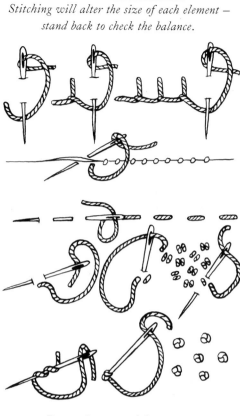

BASIC APPLIQUÉ STITCHES
*Above: blanket stitch, slipstitch, running
stitch, seed stitch, and French knots.*

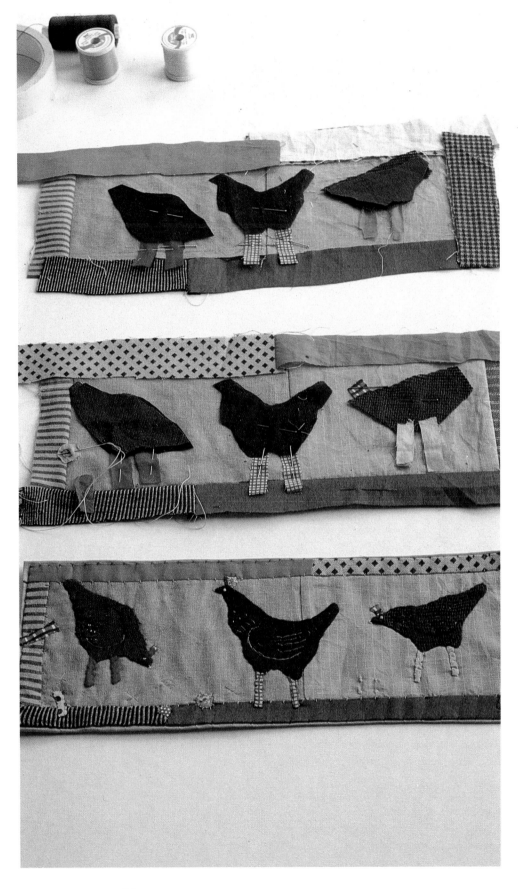

lightweight cottons) for the appliqué;
unbleached muslin or similar fabric for
the backing; a needle; cotton sewing
threads; a thimble; pins; and sharp cutting-out scissors.

The first step is to select fabrics for the
background and the borders. The
fabrics used for the background of
"Three Hens" were dyed, separately,
with onion skins and tea; a similar effect
could be achieved by using two different
beige fabrics. The two background
pieces should be machine-stitched together and the seams pressed flat. The
seam becomes an inherent part of the
picture's composition.

Cut the border strips to the desired
size, adding a little extra for turning,
and lay in place. The hens' bodies should
then be cut freely from the fabric – not
using a template. These must be cut

SIMPLE IMAGES IN A PLAIN SETTING
White mountings and wooden frames (right)
complement the childlike simplicity
of these pictures. Recurring themes are
immediately apparent.

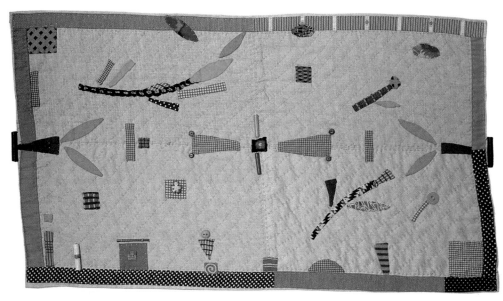

THE ELEMENTS OF APPLIQUÉ
In addition to simple abstract and figurative
patterns, appliqué can be embellished with
quilting, embroidery, and beading.

larger than the finished image to allow for turning under the raw edges. Pin the borders and the hens in place. When the balance and color seem satisfactory, machine-stitch the borders to the background fabric with right sides facing, and carefully turn under the ends of the overlapping strips.

The next stage is to refine the figurative and abstract elements of the composition into a pleasing whole. Decisions have to be made about the position of the hens in relation to each other, the color of their legs, whether to add a cockscomb and what other elements are required to complete the picture. It may be useful to pin it to a bulletin board or some other flat surface where it is possible to study the piece for some time before beginning sewing.

Sew the hens' bodies first, using ordinary sewing thread. The thread could be black or a contrasting color, to add extra interest. With a hen pinned exactly in place, sew it to the background with slipstitch, using the needle to turn under the edge. Attach all the other elements to the background in the same way. Press each one after sewing with a medium iron and a press cloth; do not press the work directly.

Baste the picture to the backing cloth around the edges and at several points across its width. Turn under the outer edges of the border and slipstitch them in place. Work additional stitches to suggest the eyes, beaks, and feathers — this will also anchor the picture to the backing cloth. Simple stitching along the outer edges of the border will add interest. The picture is now ready to be mounted and framed.

CUTTING AND MEASURING
*A piece of fabric three times the width of the
finished panel is usually required.*

EASY PLEATING
*Fabric can be gathered quickly and evenly
using a pleating machine.*

supple enough to be pleated. The use of a patterned fabric, such as a regular check, stripe, or dot, may eliminate the need to mark the gathering lines, but only if the pattern corresponds exactly to the fabric grain (as with a woven check or stripe) because printed patterns are often irregular. In England, the embroidery is traditionally done in a matching thread color, but there is no hard and fast rule. An embroidery thread, such as pearl cotton or brilliant cotton is most suitable. Smocking is usually done before the garment is assembled, and the cloth is cut approximately three times the width of the finished panel.

Other materials required for smocking are a sheet of transfer dots, strong thread for gathering, and a crewel needle. The gathering thread should preferably be of a contrasting color, so that it is visible and can serve as a guide for working the smocking stitches. Pleating machines, such as the one shown, are useful but represent a considerable outlay for anyone but the most dedicated smocker.

Before transfers were available, smockers used to have to count vertical and horizontal threads in order to mark the cloth with a grid of dots indicating the gathering lines. Although very time-consuming, this method ensured that the rows of gathering stitches corresponded exactly to one another. If transfers are used, they should be placed on the wrong side of the fabric with the lines of dots running along the warp and weft. An iron set at a cool temperature is then applied to the transfer. Care should be taken that the dots do not show through to the right side of the cloth. In the case of delicate or transparent materials, it is advisable to place a layer of cheesecloth between the cloth and the transfer to absorb superfluous ink. The dots should be spaced between ¼–½ in (5 mm–1.2 cm) apart horizontally and between ½–¾ in (1.2–2 cm) apart vertically. It is the distance between the gathering stitches that determines the width of the pleat – the wider the space, the deeper the pleat, and the more material required.

Each row of gathering requires enough thread for the width of the cloth to be smocked, leaving a loose tail at one end and a stout anchoring knot at the other. A new thread is required for each row. When all the rows for a panel have been stitched, they are carefully drawn up one at a time. The gathering is first

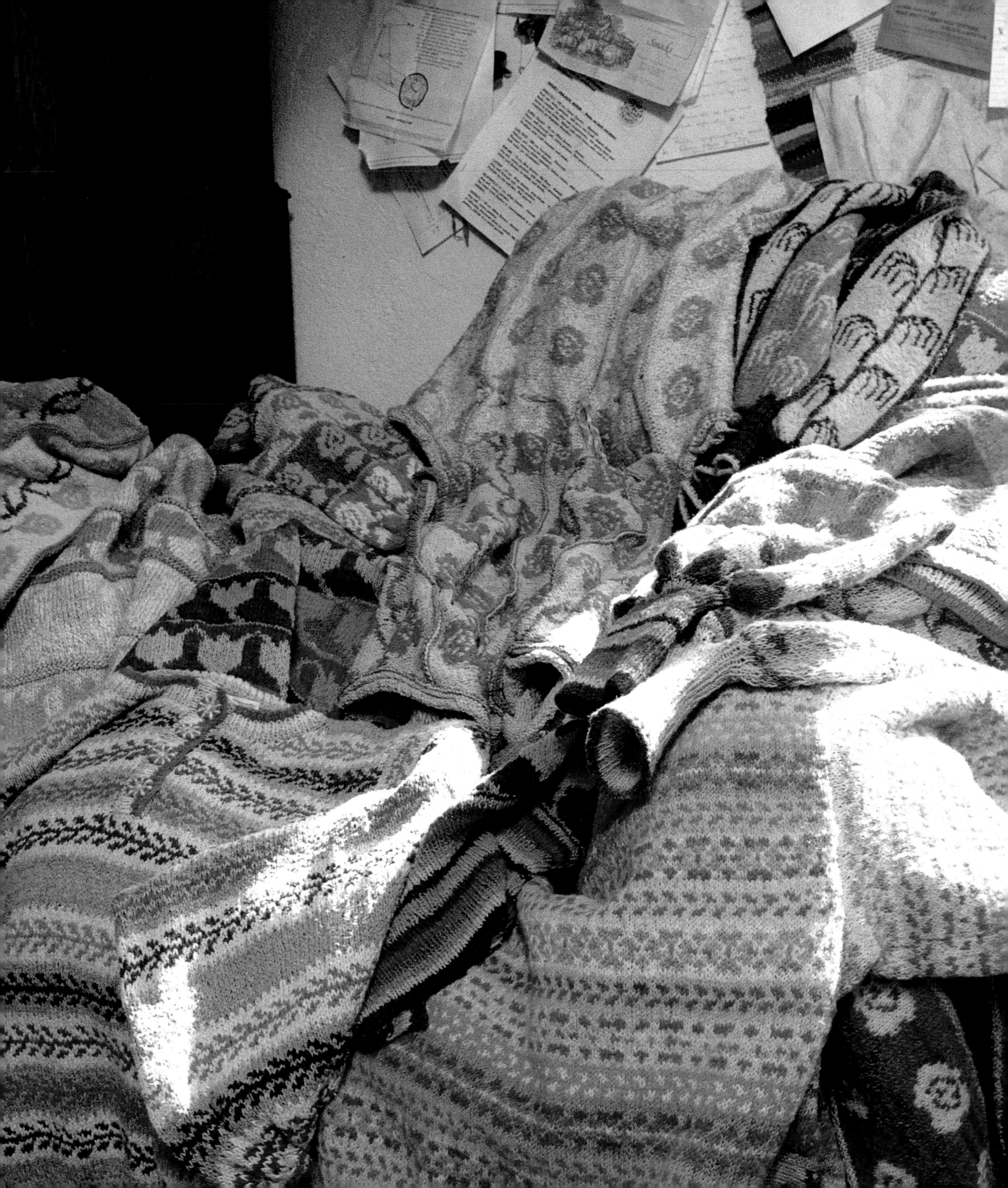

DYEING AND KNITTING

NATURALLY DYED BY DESIGN
*The subtle shades of naturally dyed yarn
complement traditional and contemporary
hand-knitted designs.*

THE NATURAL WORLD IS RICH IN potential dyes. The roots, flowers, and fruits of many plants, as well as tree bark, can be used to color cloth. In many societies these materials are used to decorate the body, too. The ancient Greeks extracted a strong purple from shellfish; it was such a laborious process that purple was worn only by the rich, and indeed is still associated with royalty. Today the only common, non-vegetable, natural dye is the red that comes from the cochineal beetle.

The origins of dyeing are hard to trace because of the perishable nature of cloth, but the earliest known examples are probably Minoan. Most of the natural dyes that are used today were already known by the Middle Ages. Blue from the indigo plant, for example, is one of the earliest known

and still one of the most successful colors. The most important development in the twentieth century has been ease and reliability of transportation, which has made the whole spectrum of vegetable dyes available throughout the world, no longer just in countries where the source plants will grow.

The main attraction of natural dyes is their softness and luminosity. Both technically and aesthetically they complement wool. Hand dyeing, which often creates slight variations in the depth of color, can produce yarn that gives a subtle painterly shading to a design when knitted up. Like the natural ingredients the processes of dyeing have changed very little. There are two basic methods of dyeing yarn: one uses "adjective" dyes, the other uses "substantive" dyes. Adjective dyes need only be boiled

with the yarn to produce a fast color; substantive dyes are color-fast only when the yarn is first impregnated with a chemical, called a mordant. In the latter method, the yarn is washed, boiled up in a mordant, then immersed in the dye and boiled until the desired depth of color is achieved. Successive batches of yarn immersed in the same dyebath will give progressively lighter shades as the color is "exhausted."

The basic mordants used in dyeing are alum, tin, chrome, and iron; of the three, alum usually produces the clearest colors with wool. Handle mordants with care – many of them are poisonous. Always wear rubber gloves and a protective apron during the dyeing process. When mordants are not in use, store them safely in a dark, locked cupboard well out of the way of children.

EQUIPMENT FOR DYEING
*All the basics can be found in the kitchen, but
should then be used only for dyeing.*

REMOVING THE HANKS
*A sturdy stick can be used to extract large
hanks of yarn from the dye.*

To dye wool at home the following equipment is required: bathroom or kitchen scales, a 7½ pint (3.5 liter) stainless steel saucepan (not suitable for cooking with after use), rubber gloves, a stick for stirring, an old teaspoon, a whisk, olive oil soap, and a muslin bag.

The mordants and dyestuffs required for natural dyeing are obtainable from craft suppliers, but a good pharmacist will be able to supply the more commonly available ingredients.

To dye the yarn for the "Poppies and Pinks" jacket shown on page 51, a total of 2 lb 4 oz (1000 g) of sport-weight natural, unbleached yarn is needed. This yarn can then be dyed in the following proportions: 4 oz (100 g) fuchsia, 4 oz (100 g) wine, 4 oz (100 g) red, 12 oz (350 g) pale blue, and 4 oz (100 g) green – 8 oz (250 g) should be left natural. In

the recipes given on page 50, quantities are for dyeing a 4 oz (100 g) hank of yarn (dry weight). In order to dye the large batch of blue using one dyebath, simply increase the length of time that each 4 oz (100 g) hank is left in the dye: 10 minutes for the first hank, 20 minutes for the second hank, and 30 minutes for the third hank.

Before dyeing, tie a 4 oz (100 g) hank of yarn in three or four places to prevent it from becoming tangled. To do this, divide the yarns randomly in two, and secure them together loosely with soft string using a figure-eight, and knot at one side. Wet the hank in cold water before mordanting.

For the fuchsia, wine, red, and yellow dyes (the initial preparation for green is to dye the yarn yellow) the same basic principles for mordanting apply.

Begin by warming 5 pints (2.3 liters) of water in a saucepan, until it is hand-hot. Then referring to the recipes on page 50, weigh out and add the necessary amount of mordant dissolved in a cup with a little warm water. Stir well and add a hank of wetted yarn. Bring the mixture to the boil, and simmer it for 20 minutes. Stir occasionally to prevent the yarn from becoming matted. Lift the hank out of the mordant, rinse thoroughly, and then squeeze out excess water. Discard the mordant, and wash the saucepan. Dye the yarn immediately.

To prepare a dyebath, warm another 5 pints (2.3 liters) of water in the clean saucepan and add the appropriate dyestuff (refer to recipe chart). Stir it in well and add the mordanted yarn. Bring it to the boil very slowly and hold it at a steady simmer. Lift the hank of yarn out

<u>DYED YARNS</u>
The longer the yarn is left in the dyebath the more color will be taken up.

of the dyebath with the stick occasionally, to check the intensity of the color. When the desired depth of color has been achieved, remove the yarn from the dyestuff. Wash the hank gently with olive oil soap, rinse, and hang the yarn on a clothesline to dry.

In order to dye the yarn blue – and consequently to dye the yellow yarn green – an adjective dye is prepared with woad leaves. Woad is one of the oldest plants used for natural dyes, and it is difficult to obtain; however, seeds are available, and it will grow quickly.

Tear the woad leaves into small pieces, referring to the recipe chart for

<u>NATURALLY DRIED</u>
After dyeing, the hanks of yarn are draped over a line and left to dry in the sun.

47

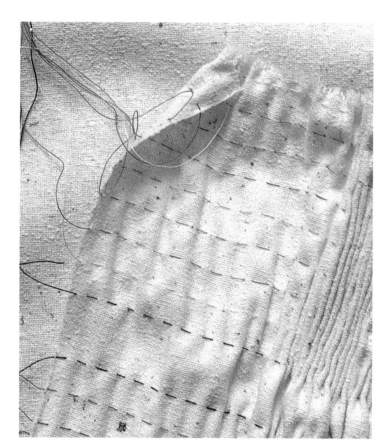

GATHERING LINES
Threads in several different colors will act as a guide for smocking.

THE FIRST ROW
A good anchoring stitch such as cable or rope stitch should be used.

drawn up tightly to straighten the folds, and the gathers stroked into even pleats, after which the gathering is relaxed to about two-thirds of the eventual width. The loose gathering threads are trimmed and tied together in pairs, and are removed only when the embroidery has been completed.

The smocking is worked on the right side of the cloth, working from left to right (except in the case of Vandyke stitch), beginning at the top left-hand corner. Left-handed smockers start at the top right-hand corner and work from right to left. The thread used for the smocking should be very securely attached and finished off because it will be subjected to stress and friction. The stitches are usually made through about one-third of the depth of each pleat. This allows for elasticity and also means

that there is no risk of the embroidery thread becoming entangled with the gathering thread.

A variety of stitches is used in smocking, including rope, cable, diamond, feather, Vandyke, chevron, honeycomb, wave, and stem stitch. These have different characteristics. Cable, for example, is a good anchoring stitch and is often used at the top or bottom of a panel of smocking. Honeycomb is a very useful stitch which can be combined with others or worked alone. Gaps between bands of smocking should not be too wide or the pleating will puff out in an unsightly way.

HAND PLEATING
Knot the ends of the thread and work even running stitches between the transfer dots.

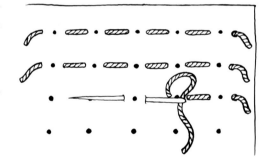

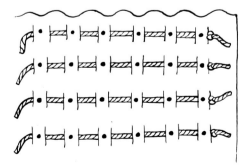

CABLE STITCH

HONEYCOMB STITCH

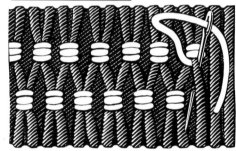

SMOCKING A PANEL
*When the rows of smocking are complete the
gathering threads can be removed.*

CABLE STITCH

This stitch forms the basis of many other smocking stitches. To keep a line of stitching straight, it is best to work along a row of gathering stitches, using the gathering thread as a guide. The effect of this stitch is achieved by holding the thread alternately above and below the needle, keeping the needle horizontal at all times.

Working from left to right, bring the needle up to the left of the first pleat; holding the thread above the needle, pick up the second pleat with a backstitch, and bring the needle up between the pleats. Join the second and third pleats in the same way, but with the thread held below the needle. Repeat the stitch across the row of gathering stitches, alternating the position of the thread on each stitch.

HONEYCOMB STITCH

Honeycomb stitch is the most elastic of all smocking stitches. Make sure that your thread is long enough to avoid unnecessary joins; three times the width of the pleated fabric is a good guide.

Stitching should be worked from left to right. Starting level with the first gathering line, bring the needle up through the first pleat. With the needle horizontal and the thread above the needle, draw the second and first pleats together with a backstitch. Work a second backstitch above the first in the same way. Work a third backstitch, bringing the needle down through the second pleat and out at the second gathering line. Join the second and third pleats with two backstitches. Work a third backstitch this time taking the needle up through the third pleat, and

bringing it out level with the first gathering line. Join the third and fourth pleats using the same sequence. Continue in this way across the row. At the end of the row, finish off the thread and start again on the left-hand side. The method is repeated across the third and fourth gathering lines. When fastening on, position the knot exactly behind the first backstitch and secure it with a small backstitch on the wrong side. Fasten off the thread on the wrong side with two backstitches under the last stitch.

VARIATIONS OF STITCH

Elaborate, intricate patterns can be achieved with a combination of smocking stitches. However, scarcely less impressive results are possible with just one or two simple stitches worked alone.

COLOR	MORDANT	DYESTUFF
FUCHSIA	1 oz (28 g) alum ½ oz (12 g) cream of tartar	1 oz (28 g) cochineal, ground into a fine powder and mixed into a paste with warm water (NB cochineal will stain)
WINE	½ oz (12 g) chrome	4 oz (100 g) Brazilwood chips (simmer for 1 hour with yarn)
RED	1 oz (28 g) alum ½ oz (12 g) cream of tartar	4 oz (100 g) Brazilwood chips (tied in a muslin bag)
BLUE	—	1 lb (450 g) woad leaves, a few drops of household ammonia and 1 teaspoon of sodium dithionite
GREEN	1 oz (28 g) alum ½ oz (12 g) cream of tartar	2 oz (55 g) weld (tied in a muslin bag); over-dye with blue dye for green

DYE RECIPES
The quantities given above are for dyeing a
4 oz (100 g) hank of yarn.

THE RAW MATERIALS
Bundles of yarn, and bags of mordants and
dyestuffs on a country dresser.

quantity. Meanwhile, bring 5 pints (2.3 liters) of water to the boil. Add the woad and boil for eight minutes. Strain and save the liquid. Cool the liquid quickly by placing the saucepan in a pan of cold water. Add the drops of ammonia, and aerate the mixture by whisking. When the froth turns blue, reheat gently until it is hand-hot. Do not simmer or overheat. Sprinkle the sodium dithionite into the mixture but do not stir. Remove the dye from the heat, and allow it to stand for five minutes. Add wet, unbleached yarn in three batches of 4 oz (100 g) to dye the yarn blue. To obtain the green yarn, place the wet yellow yarn in the dye. After approximately 20 minutes, remove the yarn, and allow it to oxidize (stand exposed to air) for 15 minutes. Wash, rinse, and dry the yarn in the usual way.

Compared to dyeing, knitting is a young craft. Evidence of early knitting, dating from the fourth and fifth centuries, has been found in Coptic tombs in Egypt, suggesting that the art originated in the East. Arab traders probably introduced the art into the Mediterranean countries in the eighth century, where knowledge spread gradually through Spain and Italy to the West.

Later examples to survive date from the late eleventh century and are all in stockette stitch, knitted either flat or in the round. By the seventeenth century knitting had become a highly organized, flourishing industry. Most knitters were men, and they became members of their guild only after an apprenticeship of six years. Even so, few new stitches seem to have been invented until the eighteenth century.

The plainness of the surface, however, encouraged knitters to experiment with color patterns. Among non-industrial knitters – many of them women making clothes for their families – quite distinctive local styles developed in different regions. One of the most famous and influential is Fair Isle, from the island of that name off the coast of Scotland. The complex multicolor patterns characteristic of Fair Isle knitting are obtained using only two colors in any one row. Unused color is stranded across the back of the patterned area to create a double thickness. Traditionally, this patterning was generally placed around the yoke, the top of the sleeves, and the lower edge of a sweater, since these were the points at which the wearer was most likely to feel the chill; the design was thus practical and decorative.

POPPIES AND PINKS JACKET

THE KIND OF SPONTANEITY TYPICAL of today's knitwear is exhibited perfectly in this beautiful "Poppies and Pinks" jacket. After a period of relative sterility, the spirit of creative experiment is returning to hand knitting. Traditional motifs, flower forms, and even paisley patterns are being used again and developed in contemporary styles. The scale of motifs is now larger, too, but the same fine yarn that was used traditionally is still favored for the intricate quality of pattern it allows.

The jacket is knitted in panels of alternating blue and cream with poppy and pinks motifs, using the Fair Isle method. The panels are separated with four rows of reverse stockette stitch in a slightly deeper blue – use the darkest of your three hanks of blue.

SIZE One size fits bust measuring 32–42 in (81–107 cm). Length from top of shoulder: 28½ in (72 cm) approximately. Width all around: 52½ in (134 cm).

MATERIALS One pair each of size 1 (2¼ mm) and 3 (3¼ mm) needles. Set of four size 1 (2¼ mm) double-pointed needles. Stitch holder. Blunt-ended tapestry needle.
Sport-weight wool: 4 oz (100 g) fuchsia; 4 oz (100 g) wine; 4 oz (100 g) red; 12 oz (350 g) pale blue; 4 oz (100 g) green and 8 oz (250 g) cream (natural). 7 buttons.

GAUGE Over color pattern on larger needles: 31 sts and 34 rows to 4 in (10 cm) square. To avoid disappointment work a sample in pattern over 36 sts for 4½ in (11 cm), then bind off and measure gauge. If gauge is too loose try a size smaller needle; if too tight, try a size larger needle.

ABBREVIATIONS K=knit; P=purl; st(s)=stitch(es); rep=repeat; beg=begin-

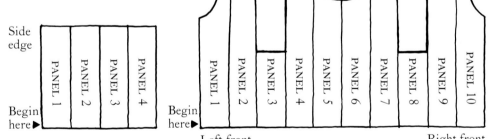

Side edge

PANEL 1 · PANEL 2 · PANEL 3 · PANEL 4

Begin here ▶

PANEL 1 · PANEL 2 · PANEL 3 · PANEL 4 · PANEL 5 · PANEL 6 · PANEL 7 · PANEL 8 · PANEL 9 · PANEL 10

Begin here ▶

Left front   Right front

	PANEL	BACKGROUND	FLOWER	STEMS
BODY	Nos 1,3,5,7,9	Cream	Red/Wine (poppies)	Green
	Nos 2,4,6,8,10	Pale Blue	Fuchsia (pinks)	Green
SLEEVES (both alike)	Nos 1 and 3	Cream	Red/Wine (poppies)	Green
	Nos 2 and 4	Pale Blue	Fuchsia (pinks)	Green
Rev st st between panels in deeper blue				

COLOR SCHEME AND ORDER OF PANELS

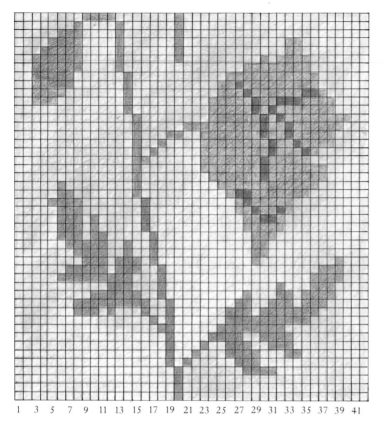

	BLUE
	CREAM
	RED
	WINE
	FUCHSIA
	GREEN

THE POPPY CHART
*Knitted from left to right, each poppy pattern
is 42 rows deep and 47 stitches across.*

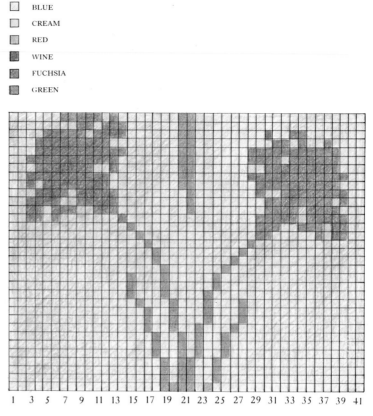

THE PINKS CHART
*Knitted from left to right, each pinks pattern
is 42 rows deep and 33 stitches across.*

ning; pat=pattern; alt=alternate; inc=increase; dec=decrease; cm=centimeters; in=inches; st st=stockette stitch; rev st st=reverse stockette stitch.

IMPORTANT When working in color pattern, weave the yarn not in use loosely over every stitch on wrong side of work. Do not pull yarn too tightly, as this will affect the gauge. Always carry yarns to the end of every row to prevent puckering. The bands of reverse stockette stitch begin with a right-side row. To give a clean edge at color change, the first row of these bands must always be a knit row.

PICKING UP STITCHES To obtain the best results stitches should always be picked up evenly. Divide the edge into four equal sections and mark with pins; then divide number of stitches required by four and pick this

number up in each section. All bound off/cast on stitches should be picked up.

BODY Using larger needles and deeper blue cast on 174 sts. Work 4 rows in rev st st. Work 12 rows of poppy repeat (47 sts) across row (you will not have a complete pat at left-hand side). Rows 1 and 2 and 41 and 42 are st st in main color.

NECK SHAPING Inc 1 st at end of K row (neck edge). Pat 3 rows. Inc 1 st at neck edge. Work 1 row. Inc 1 st at neck edge of next 6 K rows (182 sts). Work 2 rows. Cast on 15 sts at neck edge (197 sts). Work straight until 2 panels (less 1 row) have been worked, ending at neck edge.

ARMHOLE AND POCKET PLACING
Bind off 52 sts at beg of next row. Work 4 rows rev st st. Beg at lower edge work 40 sts.

Place next 40 sts on a holder. Set aside.

MAKE POCKET LINING On separate needles, cast on 40 sts and work 1 panel to match body. Return to body, work across sts of lining and pat to end. Complete underarm panel and work 3 rows rev st st. Cast on 52 sts at end of next row to complete armhole shaping. Work straight until 4 panels and 10 rows of fifth panel have been worked.

BACK NECK SHAPING Dec 1 st at neck edge on next row and then on next 2 alt rows (194 sts). Work straight until 5 panels and 26 rows of sixth panel have been worked. Inc 1 st at neck edge on next row and next 2 K rows (197 sts). Work straight until 7 pats (less 1 row) have been worked.

RIGHT ARMHOLE SHAPING AND POCKET PLACING Bind off 52 sts at neck

BUTTONING UP

*Buy or make buttons to complement the colors
and style of the jacket.*

edge, pat to end. Work 4 rows rev st st. Work 1 panel.

Make pocket top: using smaller needles cast on 40 sts and work 8 rows in rib. Leave sts on a spare needle.

Return to body, and K 40 sts, pick up sts on holder for pocket top, and place next 40 sts on holder for lining, work to end. Work 2 rows straight. Cast on 52 sts at beg of next row. Work straight until 9 panels and 11 rows of tenth panel have been worked.

FRONT NECK SHAPING Bind off 15 sts at neck edge of next row. Work 2 rows. Dec 1 st at neck edge on next 7 K rows. Work 3 rows. Dec 1 st at neck edge on next row. Work straight until tenth panel is complete, ending with 4 rows rev st st. Bind off.

POCKET LINING AND TOP Return to first pocket placed: using smaller needles rib across sts left on holder, rib 7 rows, bind off. Return to second pocket: using larger needles, work one panel across sts on holder for lining. Bind off. Slipstitch pocket linings and tops into place using the blunt-ended tapestry needle.

SLEEVES Using larger needles and cream cast on 123 sts. Work 4 complete panels ending with 4 rows rev st st. Turn cast on edge to sts on needle with right sides facing and graft together.

WRIST BANDS Using set of double-pointed needles and deeper blue, pick up 160 sts around bottom of sleeve. K3, K2 together, rep to end. K2, K2 together, rep to end. K2, K2 together, rep to end. K2, K2 together, rep to end (54 sts). Work 42 rounds in rib then rib 3 rounds in red. Bind off in fuchsia using this yarn double.

SHOULDER SEAMS Using smaller needles and pale blue, pick up 52 sts across left front shoulder. Work 4 rows rev st st. Pick up 52 sts across left back shoulder, and with right sides facing graft these sets of stitches together. Rep for right shoulder.

FRILLS AND SLEEVE INSERTION Make 3 small pleats in top of sleeve. Using set of double-pointed needles and deeper blue, pick up 110 sts around sleeve. Work 4 rounds in rev st st. Pick up sts around armhole. Place sleeve in armhole, matching underarm panels with pins, then graft together. With right side facing and using pair of smaller needles and deeper blue, pick up 92 sts around sleeve top between pins. Work 2 rows in rib. Change to red and inc in every other st (138 sts). K 1 row. Bind off in fuchsia. Rep for second sleeve.

WAIST BAND Using smaller needles and deeper blue pick up 350 sts along lower edge of body. Rib 27 rows. Change to red. Rib 2 rows. Change to fuchsia. Rib 2 rows. Bind off in double yarn.

NECK BAND Using smaller needles and deeper blue pick up 110 sts around neck edge. Rib 9 rows. P 1 row. Rib another 9 rows. Bind off. Fold band to wrong side and slipstitch in place.

FRONT BANDS Work in deeper blue.
Button band: using smaller needles pick up 220 sts down left front. Rib 9 rows. P 1 row. Rib 9 rows. Bind off. Fold band to wrong side and slipstitch in place.
Buttonhole band: pick up as for left band and rib 4 rows.
Next row: rib 6 sts * bind off 6 sts, rib 27 sts *, rep from * to * to last 16 sts, bind off 6 sts, rib to end. Rib next row casting on 6 sts over bound off sts. Rib 3 rows. P 1 row. Rib 4 rows. Rep 2 buttonhole rows. Complete to match button band.

FINISHING Weave in all ends neatly on wrong side of work. Press the pieces firmly into shape with a medium iron, using a damp cloth to protect the work. Sew the buttons firmly in place.

TASSELS AND BRAIDS

<u>ELABORATE PASSEMENTERIE</u>
The intricacy of these hand-woven braids,
fringes, ropes, cords, tufts, and tassels,
reflects their highly decorative role.

PASSEMENTERIE IS THE ALL-embracing term for the craft of making braids, fringes, cords, and tassels. On a large commercial basis, braids are power-woven, but in small firms they are often still made on hand-operated, narrow braid looms; in separate workshops cords are produced on a rope warp; and tassels are made entirely by a sequence of intricate hand operations.

Hand-woven furnishing braids and trimmings, usually designed and colored to commission, are now extremely hard to find but are becoming increasingly sought-after, especially in Europe, where they are considered an important element in traditional decor. The craft, once widely practised, is now confined mainly to Paris and London — two centers of interior decoration where there is still a steady demand for such

trimmings. A large proportion of these products are used in the restoration and re-creation of period schemes from Renaissance to Art Deco; they appear in private homes, public buildings, theaters, hotels, and historic houses across the world. Trimmings are also required for some church furnishings and for regalia used on state and royal occasions. Most often they are used for draperies, window shades, upholstery, and "wall treatments," including decorative swags and bordered panels.

A fringed braid has a number of distinct parts. Starting from the top, the first element is a fancy edging, then comes a band of plain weave which anchors the surface together. Next comes the "cobbertine" (an open structure, sometimes trellised or crocheted), then the fringe, of fine or heavy thread,

or of twisted bullion cords. This fringe can be tasseled or tufted and can incorporate flowers, rosettes, and swags. Making these tiny adornments requires considerable dexterity; from managing the multiple shuttles and manipulating the bundles of threads, to the close visual scrutiny needed to shape the loops and curves accurately.

Tassels are an important part of the output of trimmings workshops. All tassel-making is based on the same construction techniques and compositional elements: mold, skirt, ruff, and tufts. A tassel's color scheme is planned so that the main decorating color is used on the mold, a less dominant shade on the trimmings, and the heaviest color on the skirt. With all trimmings, mixed yarns in any number of colors can be used to obtain blended color effects.

THE LAYERS OF A FRINGED BRAID
*A fringe (left), is made up of a number of
distinct parts, each part interlacing to form a
complex whole.*

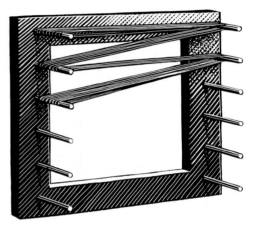

A WARPING FRAME
*The pegs are positioned so that threads of
exactly the right length can be measured out.*

To construct a tassel, a basic knowledge of making a warp on a warping
frame is required. A warping frame ensures that the tassel threads are equal in
length and held at a smooth, even tension. It is also necessary to obtain a hand-
turned, wooden, tassel mold. (Old,
deteriorating tassels can sometimes be
found in junk shops or local auctions and
dismantled for use, or a wood-turner
could be asked to replicate one.) Smooth
the mold with fine sandpaper before use.
The following materials and equipment
will also be needed: a spool rack, a warping paddle, 10 reels of fine mercerized
cotton (each reel holding about 500 yds
[500 m] of thread), two table clamps, a
reel of matching linen thread, a darning
needle, a thin piece of smooth plywood
4 x 8 in (10 x 20 cm), a reel of fuse wire,
and a fine knitting needle.

TANTALIZING TASSELS
*Large-scale tassels are increasingly employed
by interior designers.*

ACORNS AND BOWS
*Handmade tassels have been incorporated into
the design of this fringe.*

To prepare the threads for the tassel cover, wind a warp of fine cotton containing 50 ends (threads) measuring 39 in (1 m) onto a warping frame. Attach the table clamps to the side of a table, spaced about 8 in (20 cm) apart. Tie one end of the warp threads to one of the clamps. Then wind the warp in a figure-eight around the two clamps to form a smooth hank of cotton threads. Make sure that the warp is not knotted.

To cover the tassel mold with the warp, first thread a darning needle with 39 in (1 m) of linen thread. Bind the end of the linen thread firmly round the loose end of the warp. Hold the mold in one hand, and position the bound warp end at the base of the mold. Spread and carefully smooth the threads up over a section of the mold. Then pass the needle up through the central hole.

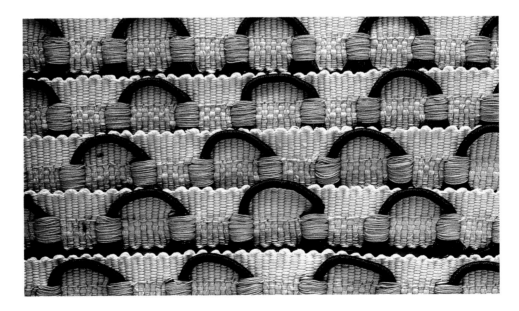

MODERN BRAIDS
*Although much of the work is traditional,
there is enormous potential for new ideas.*

COVERING THE TASSEL MOLD
*With the mold held in one hand, the warp is
carefully spread over the outside.*

FORMING THE SKIRT
*Fuse wire, a length of warp, and a plywood
batten are used to make the skirt.*

Hook the needle over the covering threads and pass it back through the central hole, drawing the covering threads in tightly (see illustration, right). Repeat this process, working counterclockwise round the mold (covering a little more of the mold each time) until the mold is completely covered and the threads are evenly spread out. Finish at the base with a knot and cut off the remaining end. Then bind two cotton threads 20 times round the groove at the base of the mold.

Prepare a warp for the skirt of the tassel. The warp should be composed of 100 ends (threads) of fine cotton measuring 4 yds (3.6 m) in length. Wind the warp around the table clamps. Cut a 39 in (1 m) length of fuse wire and fold it in half. Knot the wire, at the folded end, to the loose end of the warp.

To form the skirt, hold the wired warp end at the top of the plywood batten, with the two ends of fuse wire hanging either side of the batten. Wind the warp once round one end of the batten to form a loop 4 in (8 cm) long. Cross the wire ends over each other to enclose the top of the loop tightly. Repeat the winding and enclosing process until there are enough loops to form a skirt approximately 6 in (15 cm) in length. Finish by binding the wire around the end of the warp. Trim the end of the warp. Slide the skirt loops carefully off the batten. Wrap the skirt several times around the mold, then twist the ends of the wire together. Cut off the surplus wire. Bind the top of the skirt with a linen thread.

Next, prepare ruffs to decorate the neck of the mold. Prepare the ruff using the same method as for the skirt (see illustration, right). Wind a warp containing 15 ends (threads) 8½ yds (7.75 m) long. Use a fine knitting needle, instead of the batten. The ruff should be long enough to wrap around the neck of the mold three times. Slide the ruff off the knitting needle. Bind it around the top of the skirt firmly and secure by twisting the wire and cutting off the surplus. Cut and trim the loops at the bottom of the tassel. Finally, bind the neck of the tassel three times around using a linen thread.

Sometimes, before the ruff is attached, tasseled bullion tags are hung around the neck of the tassel.

TWO BASIC TECHNIQUES
*Covering a mold with the warp using linen
thread (a), and making a ruff (b).*

<u>ATTACHING THE SKIRT</u>
*The skirt is wrapped around the mold several
times, and secured with wire.*

<u>DECORATING THE TASSEL</u>
*A contrasting ruff and tasseled bullion tags
add final decorative detail.*

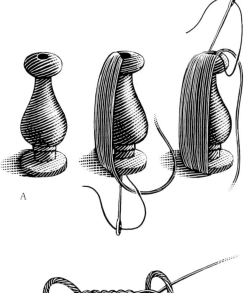

IKAT WEAVING

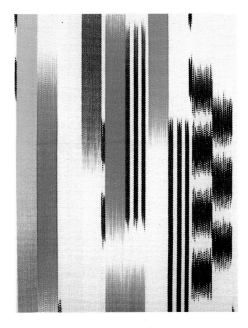

<u>WEAVING IN STRIPES</u>
*This distinctive style of weaving is intriguing
because the pattern is inherent in the weave.*

IN WOVEN CLOTH THE PATTERN AND texture are usually formed by the interplay of warp and weft – the warp threads run the length of the fabric and the weft threads from side to side. At its most basic level weaving consists of weaving the weft over and under the warp thread; the next thread passes over and under the alternate warp threads and is beaten down to hold the first one in place. There are endless permutations of this interplay which can produce rich and complex fabrics. For weavers with some experience of a four-shaft table loom, ikat weaving can provide an interesting and satisfying development of basic weaving skills. It depends on placing pattern in the warp threads – the weft merely gives the cloth structure, thus making it possible to achieve stunning effects with a plain weave.

Ikat weaving is an ancient technique in which the pattern of the cloth is achieved by tie-dyeing parts of the warp before threading it onto the loom. It is a process that is as much about dyeing and pattern-making as it is about weaving.

The warp is dyed in sections, carefully and accurately following a pre-determined design. The weaving itself is often a simple, plain weave using the dominant color from the pattern for the weft. There is also a tradition of double ikat, in which a pattern is created by tie-dyeing both warp and weft, but examples of such work are rare.

Ikat is made in many countries in Asia, South America and Africa. However, there is no recognized tradition of ikat in either North America or Europe, with the exception of some two-color designs produced in Majorca, mainly as furnishing fabrics. The textile industries of the West have tried to imitate the ikat style by printing, rather than dyeing, the warp.

Each culture that practices the craft has its own word for it: "ikat" is a Malayan word which means to "tie" or "bind" and describes the technique.

Ikat can be practiced using any yarn – usually cotton, silk, or wool – but because it is such a time-consuming process, it has often been used to produce high-quality textiles, which is why silk predominates. There are examples from Central Asia in which the warp has been tied and dyed up to seven times. The very fine silk *patolas* of Gujarat are double ikats. These intricate, gossamer sari lengths were once so highly prized that they served as currency and were considered more valuable than gold.

AN IKAT BOOKMARK
The warp has been transferred to the loom and the pattern develops before your eyes.

Today, commercial pressure has resulted in much more simplified ikats, which rely for their effect on powerful color combinations.

Traditionally, ikat is produced by a team of highly skilled specialists: tiers, dyers, warpers, and weavers. This is still the case in some regions. In Central Asia, at the height of ikat production, the dyeing itself was specialized, with cold dyehouses for indigo and hot dyehouses for reds and yellows; shades in between were achieved by overdyeing.

The traditional weavers work with patterns that have been handed down the generations and learned during the making process. These designs are not committed to paper; the pattern is tied directly into the warp from memory. For the contemporary weaver the attraction of the process is the constant dis-

<u>DYEING AND PATTERNING</u>
*The stunning effects are achieved by dip-
dyeing and tie-dyeing the warp in sections.*

covery of *new* patterns and color combinations. The design process takes
place on paper, though some coloring
may be decided at the dyeing stage, particularly with dip-dyeing – where colors
overlap and merge there is always an element of chance.

The pattern is put into the warp in
sections usually measuring ¼–2 in
(5–50 mm) wide. It would be difficult
to tie a thicker section satisfactorily. Designs are, therefore, composed largely
of vertical lines with color used in
vibrating contrasts. Carefully worked
out juxtapositions create a sense of
movement. To this end, shocking pink

<u>FOUR-SHAFT TABLE LOOM</u>
*The ikat bookmark (opposite) was woven on
this straightforward, small-scale loom.*

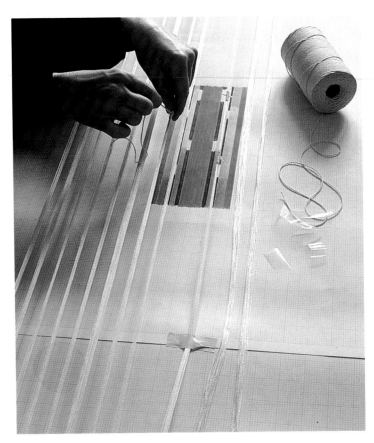

BINDING THE WARP

Threads are stretched across the design and sections to be tie-dyed bound tightly.

TIE-DYEING

After dyeing, the soft string binding is removed to reveal the undyed sections.

DIP-DYEING IN SECTIONS

Interesting juxtapositions of color arise where colors merge.

is often set against primary reds and yellows, using a combination of tie- and dip-dyeing techniques.

Fine silk is one of the most satisfying threads to work with, as it takes dye brilliantly and permits finer detail in the patterning. An ikat effect could be achieved either by printing or by painting but what gives the cloth its special quality is the fact that the pattern is an inherent part of the fabric – color, pattern, and structure are one.

To make the bookmark shown opposite, you must have a basic knowledge of weaving on a four-shaft table loom. Materials and equipment needed are: spun silk yarn 100/4s (thicker yarn may be used); acid dyes in a range of bright colors; a four-shaft table loom; warping pegs; clear plastic (freezer bags cut into pieces will do); soft cotton string; suitable pots for dyeing; and graph paper ruled in 1 in (2.5 cm) squares.

The bookmark is a mirror-image design with a broad central section in the dominant color, blue. The pattern is first worked out on graph paper. This yarn produces 100 threads to 1 in (2.5 cm), so with ten squares to every 1 in (2.5 cm) on the graph paper, one square equals 10 warp threads. The finished bookmark measures 3½ in (9 cm) wide by 10 in (25 cm) long.

The 360 warp threads are arranged as follows, left to right: 30 blue; 40 dip-dyed in red, yellow, and turquoise; 10 tie-dyed black; 30 dip-dyed colors as before; 20 tie-dyed black; 100 blue; 20 tie-dyed black; 30 dip-dyed colors as before; 10 tie-dyed black; 40 dip-dyed colors, as before; 30 blue. Draw this color sequence on the graph paper.

WEAVING THE BOOKMARK
*Use a plain weave and beat the weft down
firmly for a beautiful finish.*

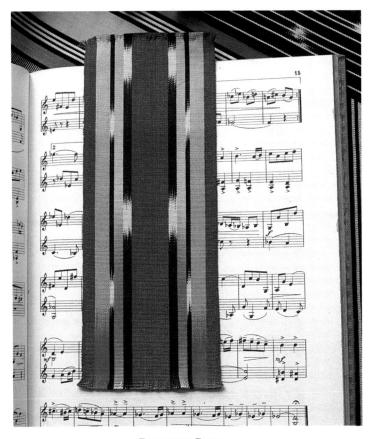

PRACTISE PIECE
*Making a bookmark is a perfect way to learn
the principles of ikat weaving.*

Prepare a warp 2 yds (1.8 m) long for each of the color sections, using warping pegs in the normal way to form a cross. A warp of this length will make as many as five bookmarks. It is very important to keep the tension even. When all sections have been wound, they are brought together and stretched across a flat surface, with the tension held.

Place the graph paper design under the warp; it will indicate the sections of the warp that must be tied. Where a white patch occurs in the black section, an equivalent amount on the warp must be bound very tightly with fine cotton string to ensure that no dye enters; a strip of clear polyethylene placed beneath the binding is very effective in this respect. Bind the area twice and secure the binding with a firm knot. If plastic is used in the binding, the warp must only be simmered in the dyebath; rapid boiling would melt the plastic.

The next stage is to dye each section of the warp: the blues, the tie-dyed blacks, then the dip-dyed sections. Dye a small hank of the same yarn blue for the weft.

For the dip-dyed sections, prepare three dyes. The stronger the solution of acid dye the more intensely it will penetrate the yarn. Dyes for dipping must always be boiled.

Dip equal sections of the warp into the first color; leave them in for one minute; then rinse them out under cold running water and squeeze them in a towel to remove excess moisture. Then dip the warp into the second color. Interesting secondary colors will occur where the two meet. Rinse and squeeze out these sections, then dip them into the third color and rinse thoroughly. This can be a messy process; time, concentration, and old clothes are required.

The dyed warps must be allowed to dry thoroughly before the tied sections are unwrapped. The warp is then raddled (spread to the correct width) and wound onto the loom. At this stage it is important to have assistance, so that the warps can be stretched and held under accurate tension while being wound onto the roller. The assistant has to hold the ends of the warp, while it is transferred to the loom. Thread the loom in the normal way for a plain weave.

A firm weave is achieved by severely beating the weft. Because this is a dense weave, no special finishing of the ends is required. When the entire length has been woven, remove it from the loom. Cut into bookmarks and steam-press with a medium iron.

RAG RUGS

A COUNTRY TRADITION
*Making rag rugs has always been a country
pastime. A spare room could be converted into
a functional workshop.*

TURNING RAGS INTO RUGS WAS ONCE considered a thrifty occupation. For many people rugs were an important barrier against the cold, and an inexpensive way of adding comfort to their homes. During the long winter evenings families would gather in the kitchen to make mats. Old meal-sacks, which were attached to a wooden frame, formed the base. By candlelight, some members of the household would cut worn-out garments into strips, while others hooked or prodded the ribbons of cloth through the burlap. When the rug was finished it would be laid in the place of honor in the parlor, and an older one would be relegated to a bedroom or the kitchen. Unfortunately, hardly any of these old rugs have survived, because necessity dictated that they be used until they were completely worn out.

The decline of the rag rug began in the first part of this century. Gradually wall-to-wall carpets became easily affordable, and rag rugs became somewhat superfluous. Today, with the growing concern for conservation and the recycling of materials, rag rugs have made a comeback, and the few nineteenth-century rugs to have survived have now become collectors' items.

There are several ways of making rag rugs. The early American settlers originally braided their spent cloth and coiled it to form a flat mat. Once jute (the raw material from which burlap is made) began to be imported, they adopted hooked and prodded techniques, resembling those used in the North of England, although the braided rugs continued to be made and are still very popular. In Scandinavian countries

rag rugs are usually woven on looms.

Prodded rugs are made from small rectangles, or "clippings," of fabric, creating a thick pile with a shaggy appearance; with this technique designs are restricted to stripes or marbled effects. Hooked rugs, using long strips of cloth, have a close, looped pile, ideal for pictorial motifs and fine color shading. Americans and Swedes have always taken great care to embellish their mats, making them objects of beauty. Some rugs portray simple scenes of everyday life – the home, favorite pets or vases of flowers – whereas others copy patterns taken from old quilts, lace curtains, wallpaper, tiles, or mosaics; a few others have abstract designs. It is harder to create a pattern in woven rugs than in hooked ones, but interesting designs can be achieved by tying strips of cotton,

The Hooked Rug

Pattern can be worked into the squares or
they can be left plain.

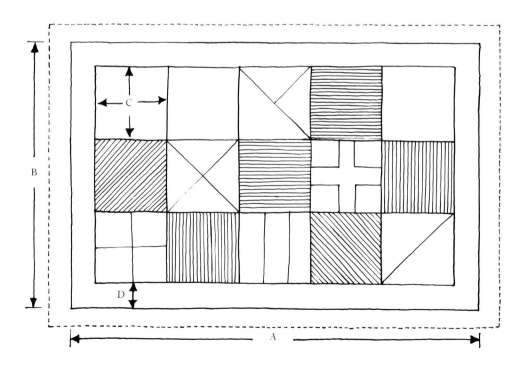

rayon, wool, or silk onto the warp as the weaving progresses. In the work of many contemporary hooked rug designers, the colors fuse together, almost resembling an Impressionist painting.

To make a hooked rug, collect as many different types and colors of rags as possible. Possible sources include old bed linen, tweed jackets, flannel trousers, cotton dresses, floral blouses, aprons, damask tablecloths, towels, and old sweaters; the greater variety collected, the greater scope there is for random effects with color and texture. Rummage sales and remnant counters are an inexpensive source of scraps.

Dimensions And Design

A = 34 in (86 cm), B = 22 in (56 cm),
C = 6 in (15 cm), D = 2 in (5 cm).

CUTTING THE FABRIC
Strips should be cut as long as possible from a wide variety of fabrics (right).

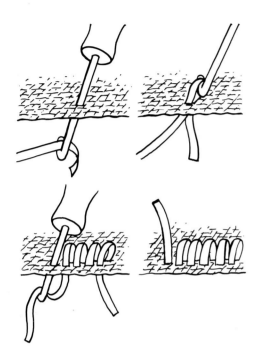

THE HOOKING TECHNIQUE
Push the hook down through the burlap, catch the strip, and bring it up to form a loop.

Avoid materials that fray excessively. Once all the rags have been assembled, cut them into long strips, about ⅝ in (1.5 cm) wide; finer fabrics should be cut wider to maintain an even density so that the rug lies flat. Divide the strips of rag into their different colors and hang them up or drape them over a towel rack; if a large mat is going to be worked, roll them into balls – but keep them nearby for inspiration.

A rug hook is the only special tool needed. A local craft group should be able to provide the address of a supplier and old ones can sometimes be found in junk shops. An alternative is to use a

MAKING THE RUG
Begin work at the center of the rug, the weave should be as dense as possible.

UNDERSIDE VIEW
*The ends of the strips are on the top of the
rug, which gives the back a good finish.*

very large crochet hook. A waterproof marker or a wax crayon is used to mark the design. A rectangular quilting frame will make working easier.

The backing should be a loosely-woven fabric; burlap is ideal because the hook can be freely pushed through the weave. Alternatively, meal-sacks can still be acquired from grocery and health food stores and put to use. Hooked rag rug making is a slow process, so it is a good idea to start with a small mat or window-seat cushion. The small rug shown on page 68 is made from half a meal-sack and measures 34 x 22 in (86 x 56 cm). A whole sack will make a long runner for a corridor, or a seat pad for a wooden settle.

If you are using a sack, first unpick the seams and machine stitch or hem the raw edges to prevent them from fray-ing. Once this is done, draw the design onto the backing with a waterproof marker or a wax crayon. The rug can either be made up as shown on page 68, or simple motifs could be drawn in each section. Alternatively, create a repeat pattern by making a cardboard template and use it as a guide.

If you are working without a frame, work from the center out, in order to maintain an even tension and prevent the base from becoming misshapen. If the rug is attached to a frame, work from side to side and top to bottom. In either case, work with the right side of the rug facing up.

Hold a length of the fabric strip on the underside of the burlap with one end just under the starting point. Push the hook down through the cloth at a slight angle, catch the end of the strip, and pull it through to the other side. Make the next hole as close as possible to the first, and bring up a small amount of the strip, forming a loop about ⅝ in (1.5 cm) deep. Continue to the end of the strip, bringing it up to the surface to finish. Trim the end level with the loops. Start a new strip in the hole where the previous strip ended. At the edge, turn the fabric and work through both layers for a tidy hem.

To develop skill and speed, it is worthwhile starting with a simple geometric design, progressing to more pictorial subjects involving curved lines on oval, circular, or triangular bases.

SCRAPS OF COLOR
*The strips of colored rag can be woven in
stripes, bands, or fused randomly.*

SMOCKING

<u>DECORATIVE DETAIL</u>
*As well as traditional panels of smocking,
embroidery can be worked on the cuffs and
collar of a garment.*

Smocking, a form of embroidery in which decorative stitching is applied to a ground of evenly pleated cloth, provides an ingenious solution to the age-old problem of how to make a garment fit snugly without constricting movement. A smocked panel in a garment reduces fullness without being rigid or bulky and gives wide scope for ornamental virtuosity.

The Anglo-Saxon word *smoc* referred to the under-garment worn by women in the Middle Ages and corresponds to the Old French word *chemise*. Some of these early smocks were pleated and embroidered at neck and cuff, thus giving shape to what would otherwise have been a simple, square-cut garment.

In England, the countryman's smock, often thought to have been traditional farm-laborers' wear for hundreds

of years, was actually in popular use only from the mid-eighteenth century to the mid-nineteenth century. This was a loose-fitting garment with sleeves which was put on over the head and extended to the knee. Smock-frocks, as they were called in the nineteenth century, were generally made of coarse materials, sometimes waterproofed with linseed oil, and with simple embroidered decoration for everyday use; finer fabrics with more elaborate embellishment characterized smocks for Sunday wear. Beads were sometimes incorporated in the embroidery. The Industrial Revolution brought the demise of the home-made smock-frock. Unemployment drove farm-workers to the towns, where they soon learned that the smock-frock marked them as country-bumpkins and discarded it as soon as they could.

Nevertheless, the decline of the smock-frock was mourned by many, and its picturesqueness was celebrated in art and literature. Interest in smocking was revived by the Arts and Crafts Movement, and in the 1890s smocks were promoted as "aesthetic" dress for children. Since then, the popularity of smocking, particularly on children's clothes, has never declined.

There are two consecutive stages in traditional smocking; the pleating of the cloth and the decorative stitching that holds the pleats in place. In the first stage it is important that the pleats are accurately aligned with the grain of the cloth; in the second, that the stitching allows for a certain degree of elasticity in the finished panel. A variety of fabrics is suitable for smocking, the principal criterion being that the cloth should be

PAPER CRAFTS

PAPERMAKING □ PAPERMARBLING □ CALLIGRAPHY

WOOD ENGRAVING □ LETTERPRESS PRINTING

BOOKBINDING □ PAPIER MÂCHÉ

PAPERMAKING

DECORATIVE HAND-MADE PAPER
*Infinite varieties of paper can be made on
very simply constructed wooden frames,
known as "molds."*

ECONOMIC NECESSITY HASTENED the invention of paper, which is usually credited to a Chinese court official named Ts'ai Lun in AD 105. Paper served as a considerably cheaper, though less permanent, alternative to silk as a surface for writing and painting. Today, almost two thousand years later, it is still an indispensable and inexpensive means of transmitting and preserving information, including this book. But paper has had its other uses; for example, it was used to make sliding screens, fans, and kites.

From China, knowledge of papermaking slowly reached Korea and Japan, while, via the trade routes, paper also arrived in Egypt. There, the use of cotton cloth as raw material by local papermakers resulted in a denser, more opaque paper than the Oriental counter-part. This Egyptian tradition of papermaking eventually reached Spain from where it spread gradually to each country in Europe, and across the Atlantic to Spanish America. Paper was being made in Mexico almost a century before the craft was launched in North America, in 1690.

Increasingly voracious demands for paper motivated the search for even cheaper bulk raw materials. During the eighteenth century, it was discovered that wood fulfilled this need, being plentiful and easily available. As papermaking became mechanized, trees became the staple raw material for the industry, and they remain so today, though hemp and flax are still used to make better-quality paper for important documents.

Mechanized papermaking still follows the same basic procedures employed by the earliest Chinese paper-makers. Soaking vegetable matter in water disentangles the short fibers of which it is composed. When a mesh is dipped into the resulting pulp, the liquid drains through the mesh, leaving a layer of fibers which, when dried, interlace again to form a thin, flexible sheet of paper.

Papermaking by hand, in small quantities, has continued to serve the special needs of artists working in watercolors and fine art printmakers. But apart from the work of a few dedicated individuals, hand papermaking has languished during this century. In recent years, though, a renaissance of the craft has been evident, particularly in the United States, not only for fine printing and bookbinding, but as a medium in its own right – the "paper art object."

<u>A Delicate Mesh Of Fibers</u>
*Be careful not to disturb the surface of the
mold as it is lifted out of the pulp.*

<u>Air-drying The Paper</u>
*A number of sheets of paper can be made in
one batch. Dry them at a slight angle.*

<u>Papermaking At Home</u>
Equipment is easily obtainable.

Using household kitchen equipment, free or very cheap raw materials and relatively little working space, it is possible to make an amazing variety of papers by hand. The sheet of decorative paper described here incorporates dried fern fronds, and is made simpler but no less effective by using recycled paper as its basic material.

Good-quality scrap paper is discarded every day by printers, and suitable waste paper can also be acquired free from many offices. Computer print-out paper is particularly suitable. Newspaper should not be used because it soon discolors, and glossy magazines should also be avoided. If paper has been printed or written upon, the ink will lend a slight tint to the pulp.

For this paper you will need a handful of small pressed and dried fern fronds, a

PEELING FROM THE MOLD
Use a sharp palette knife to lift a corner of
the paper, then peel away carefully.

SPECIAL TOUCHES
Petals, tiny leaves and even specks of gold
leaf add decorative detail.

kitchen blender, a bucket, a rectangular plastic dishwashing bowl, a thin-bladed palette knife, and a simple wooden frame smaller than the dishwashing bowl (this could be an old picture frame). You will also need a piece of glass curtain fabric to stretch across the frame and a stapler or some thumbtacks for attaching it.

Soak the waste paper in a bucket of water until it is thoroughly softened. Depending upon the kind of paper used, this could take anything from one hour to two days. In the meantime, prepare the frame by stretching the glass curtain fabric over it and stapling or tacking it in place; this prepared frame is called a "mold." When the paper pulp has reached the required consistency, place a handful of it, about the size of an egg, into a kitchen blender three-quarters full of water (cold or warm). Resist the temptation to put in too much paper.

Run the blender while counting to 20, then check that a homogeneous liquid has formed. If any bits of paper remain, run the blender again for half the time. Make about six blender loads, putting five of them into the plastic dishwashing bowl, and keeping one aside to add to the bowl as the level of the pulp becomes depleted. Then add the fern fronds to the main batch.

Wet the fabric surface of the mold by rubbing a wetted hand over it; this helps the pulp to drain. Dip the frame vertically into the pulp at the far end of the bowl and then slide it so that it is horizontal under the surface of the pulp. Draw it through the pulp, scooping up the ferns randomly, and lift it out of the pulp, holding it horizontal. Give it a little shake and allow it to drain. Try to prevent drips from your hands from falling onto the surface of the mold.

Lay the frame on a piece of newspaper to finish draining, then, after about an hour, place it in a covered, sheltered spot outdoors, tilted at an angle, so that it can dry more quickly. When the paper is perfectly dry (this can take up to 24 hours), peel it from the mold with the palette knife.

Ferns are only one of many things that can be incorporated successfully with pulp in this way to make highly individual hand-made papers. Other suitable objects include pressed flowers and leaves, cut or punched-out colored confetti, and small pieces of paper with words, letters, or musical notes printed on them – the possibilities for decorating hand-made paper are limitless.

PAPERMARBLING

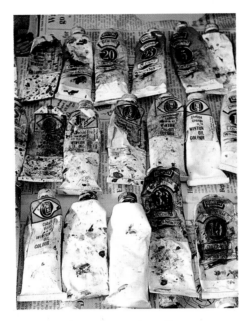

SWIRLS, FEATHERS, AND SPATTERS
*Oil paints produce soft marbled effects. The
range of patterns is only limited by the
marbler's imagination.*

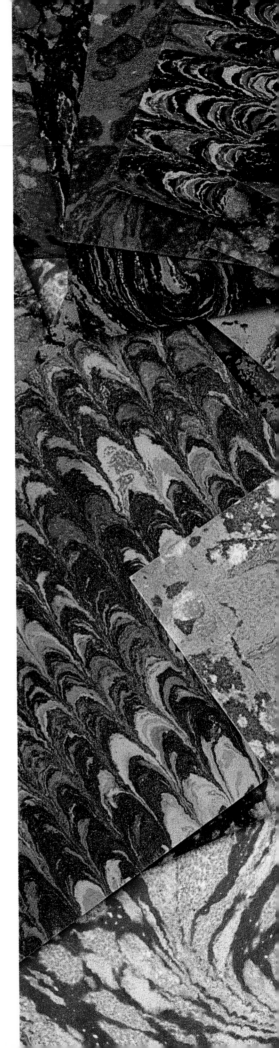

A FUNCTION OF DECORATION IS TO add value to objects; books, for example, have always been treasured both as vehicles for ideas and as objects in their own right. The addition of decorative endpapers – including marbled papers – to books was developed through the craft of bookbinding. As the name indicates, marbled papers derive their patterns – veining, spattering, feathering, and swirling – from the natural patterns of marble itself. Today, marbled papers are used to enhance a variety of objects, including gift boxes, candleshades, and lampshades as well as a range of notebooks and diaries.

The history of this craft is obscure, although it is believed to have originated in the East. Marbled papers first came to Europe (during the Crusades) via Turkey, and the Turks still maintain a reputation for fine marbling, as do the Venetians. Merchants who traveled the silk routes during the fifteenth and sixteenth centuries, brought marbling to Venice. The Venetians worked out how to marble and then guarded their secret closely. From the seventeenth to the nineteenth centuries the Venetian bookbinders sought to keep their methods to themselves by breaking up the work within their own workshops, thus ensuring that no single employee knew the whole process or the recipes. How far they succeeded is a moot point, but twentieth-century European and North American craftsmen have come up against difficulties in learning marbling techniques for themselves.

Basically, the process involves floating colored paints on thickened water and laying a sheet of paper upon the

PREPARING THE PAINT
It is very important that the paint is mixed to just the right consistency.

SPATTERING THE SURFACE
Small specks of paint must be evenly distributed across the tray.

LAYING DOWN THE PAPER
When the pattern is complete a sheet of paper captures it.

EQUIPMENT FOR PAPERMARBLING
A shallow tray, thickened water, oil paints, paintbrushes, and pattern-making implements are some of the necessities.

floating colors to catch them. When the sheet is pulled away the water is clean, and all the color is on the paper. Patterns are created by combing and feathering the colors before setting down the paper. Intricate and beguiling decorations can be created, and experienced marblers can produce more or less the same pattern time after time, although one sheet never quite replicates another.

There are two kinds of marbling: one using water-based colors, the other using oil-based colors. The water-based colors produce a very sharp image; the oil paints, a softer effect.

The materials required are relatively few and easily obtained. The sheets of paper should be absorbent, drawing or tinted paper is best; avoid heavily coated sheets. A shallow tank is required to hold the water; and the water will need

thickening with size (wallpaper paste or carrageen moss can be used). Professional marblers thicken the water with carrageen moss. The moss, or paste, adds body to the water, so that it holds the paint on its surface; the water needs to be sufficiently thick to hold the paint long enough to make a pattern and capture it on paper. Some waste paper will be needed for cleaning the tank.

The paints used here are oil paints, thinned with mineral spirit. After they have been thinned, add a few drops of ox gall (this helps the paint to spread evenly across the tank).

Good-quality ½ in (1.2 cm) paintbrushes are required, and a 1 in (2.5 cm) brush for laying down the background color is helpful. It does not matter whether the brush has nylon or natural bristles; it is important, however, that

MAKING PATTERNS
A marbling comb can be drawn across the
surface to create a variety of patterns.

USING A STYLUS
A sharp, pointed stylus, gently dragged up
and down the tray, creates a feather effect.

the bristles should not detach themselves from the brush and pockmark the pattern. For pattern-making a stylus and a marbling comb are needed.

Papermarbling requires hours of practise to achieve perfect results every time. At first, proceed by trial and error. Satisfactory results are more likely to be obtained if all the equipment is at hand: the paints should be mixed in advance; waste paper should be cut into strips; and the cold water in the tank should be thickened with the size.

A pattern is established on the water by laying down a background color and then setting three or four more colors upon it. Each color is applied by flicking it onto the water with a paintbrush. The action is all in the wrist. Spatter the background paint evenly over the surface, working methodically across and

down the tank. The paint should spread a little; if it goes into blobs or sinks, then it is too thick, so thin it with mineral spirit, or add a drop or two of ox gall. If the paint runs all over the place, either the water or the paints, or both, are too thin.

Once the background color has been laid down, further colors are spattered onto the surface according to individual taste. The mixture for the background paint should be fairly loose, but each successive color used should be slightly thicker than the preceding one. When a pleasing pattern is achieved, a sheet of paper can be set down to capture the pattern. This stage requires a deft hand.

Lay the paper upon the surface by setting down one corner of it and then gently letting the paper unroll onto the surface. Do not simply drop it onto the

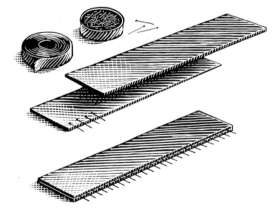

MAKING A MARBLING COMB
Cut two strips of cardboard slightly shorter
than the width of the tank and 4 in (10 cm)
deep. Tape dressmaker's pins along one of the
strips at intervals of about ½ in (1.2 cm).
Glue on the other strip, sandwiching the pins.
Varnish the card to make it waterproof.

DRYING THE PAPER
*The marbled sheets are fixed into racks and
left to dry.*

*The professional papermarbler continually
discovers new and exciting mixtures of color
and pattern. There is no end to the number
of combinations that can be achieved,
but best results are obtained using three
or four colors.*

A SWIRLING PATTERN
*The stylus can also be used to create small
whirls of color.*

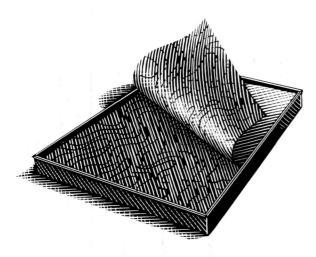

REMOVING FROM THE TRAY
*It is quite surprising how resilient a freshly-
marbled pattern is. Lift the paper from
one corner and peel gently back. Scrape it
across the edge of the tray to remove
excess size.*

surface abruptly. The action should be smooth and continuous; if it is not, hairline cracks will break up the pattern, and air bubbles will form under the surface of the paper.

Lift the paper away from the surface immediately, and scrape it across the side of the tank to remove excess size; the pattern will not be affected by this apparently brutal action. Lay the paper face up onto a sheet of waste paper; when it is dry, flatten it by pressing it under weights – heavy books will do.

Most of the paint will have been removed from the tank, except possibly around the edges. Clean this by drawing the strips of waste paper over them. The marbling process can then be repeated.

Having experimented with spatter patterning, the more adventurous techniques of feathering, swirling, and even shaking, can be attempted. For feathering, spatter the colors onto the paper in the usual way. Then run the stylus across the tank of paint from left to right several times. Draw the comb immediately across the tank in the opposite direction to the lines created by the stylus. The pattern can then be captured on a sheet of paper.

A swirling effect is also created with the stylus: dip it into the spattered paint and swirl it to make whorls, which may take the form of separate spirals or a single flowing gesture from top to bottom or side to side. Swirling and feathering can be combined to produce interesting mixtures of color and pattern. A moiré effect can be obtained by gently shaking the tank as the paper is set upon the water; this is best done by two people, working in unison.

TOOLS OF GREAT SIMPLICITY

Quills, made from goose, turkey, or swan feathers, a selection of sable paintbrushes, watercolor paints and fine paper are the basic equipment for calligraphy – the extra ingredients are discipline and imagination.

CALLIGRAPHY

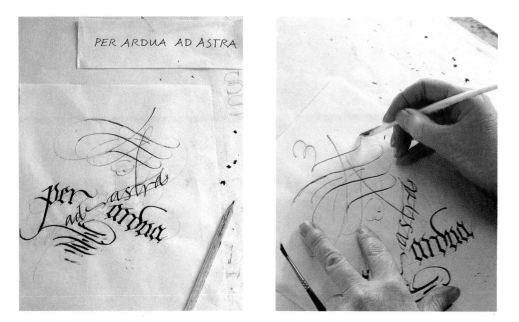

PER ARDUA AD ASTRA

PAINTING WITH WORDS
*A Latin phrase, meaning "through adversity
to the stars," is the starting point.*

THERE IS A LONG TRADITION OF hand-written documents stemming back to the invention of papyrus paper by the ancient Egyptians. Cursive writing began to flourish in ancient Rome with the introduction of papyrus from Egypt. But the high period for European calligraphy and illumination was between the seventh and eleventh centuries, when quill pens and animal-skin materials such as parchment and vellum were used to produce work of lavish detail and quality – some of which survives today. Much later, in the nineteenth century, there was another period of fine writing; the introduction of pointed metal pens in the early 1800s and the increase in office work gave another boost to the scribe's art.

Calligraphy underwent a modern renaissance at the beginning of the twentieth century, when a Scotsman, Edward Johnston, began studying early manuscripts and illuminated books. He became fired with a passion for lettering; his writings on the subject and his letter designs are still worth studying.

Calligraphy, and lettering generally, is a disciplined but expressive form of drawing. Like any art, calligraphy has its rules, and although they are not absolute, they form a basis for the construction of letters. For example, the contrast between thick and thin lines is produced not by pressure but by the direction in which the nib is pulled. Note, too, that the pen or quill is (nearly) always pulled, not pushed; a pushed pen grates, splutters, and blurs the lines. The angle at which the pen is held must remain constant. The general rule for the order of strokes that make up a letter is from top to bottom and from left to right.

Brushes, pens with steel nibs, and quills will make the marks, and vellum, hand-made paper, watercolor paper, drawing paper, and layout paper can all receive them. Layout paper is useful for practice and designing because it enables the calligrapher to test the compositions against one another.

Gesso is used for works of calligraphy illuminated with gold. To achieve the bright, mirror-like appearance of gold illumination, a cushion of gesso is required on the writing surface to receive the gold leaf. The gesso must be hard enough to burnish but flexible enough not to crack; and it must become slightly sticky when breathed upon, to enable the gold leaf to stick. Above all the mixture must be smooth so that the gold will reflect as much light as possible.

WORKING UP AN IDEA
*The calligrapher practices on layout paper to
achieve the right balance.*

The ingredients required for calligrapher's gesso are: 16 parts slaked plaster (dental), 6 parts white lead, 2 parts sugar, 1 part fish glue, a pinch of Armenian bole and a little distilled water.

All these ingredients are ground together with the distilled water until they form a smooth, thick cream. This is poured into a container and allowed to dry. It is then stored until needed.

The motto *Per ardua ad astra* ("through adversity to the stars") has been used for the sample of calligraphy shown. In this example *Per ardua* is a weighty gothic script done in dark blue watercolor paint using a steel-nibbed pen. The spiky gothic letters, together with the emphatic flourish beneath them, suggest the harshness of adversity – unlike *ad astra* whose graceful italic script (done with a quill, using light blue watercolor) leaps up in a joyful flourish to touch the illuminated stars.

This piece of calligraphy has been executed on vellum. For practice, begin with layout paper, and progress later to drawing paper, or vellum, if the work is to be illuminated. If vellum is used it should first be rubbed lightly with fine sandpaper.

Rather than draw a grid and seek to copy this example precisely, it is better to look hard at the letters and practice them freehand. Calligraphy and lettering are about rhythm; the swings that sweep through a line and the follow-through are important.

For instance, take the letter 'P' as a starting point and analyze the strokes of which it is composed. There is the first stroke, a long pull-down of the main stem; and then the strokes that compose the body, not neglecting the serif at the top or the angular pair of strokes that bisect the tail. The change in line from thin to thick of the gothic letter, which produces its dramatic quality, can be practised by sweeping and flicking the pen across and slightly up, and then turning back upon yourself and down. Imagine that the movement in the line is in the wrist, and all manner of rhythms become possible.

Using the quill for the italic *ad astra*, practise the letter "t." It starts high in the heavens, but the flourish to which it is connected is a separate, but continuous, stroke (obliging you to break the rule of not pushing the quill).

The stars were done last. If gold illumination is to be used, take the dry gesso and reconstitute it with a little distilled water until it achieves the con-

ADDING GOLD LEAF
*Gilding illuminates a composition. The
application requires a delicate touch.*

sistency of thick ink. Feed the gesso with a brush into a quill, and draw with it directly on the piece. When the gesso has dried, remove irregularities with a sharp knife. To gild the surface, first breathe on the gesso to make it sticky, then apply gold leaf, either with the tip of the forefinger or with a gilder's tip (see page 175). Burnish it gently with a burnishing tool (an agate stone set in a handle). Brush off any excess with a clean watercolor brush. Yellow watercolor paint could be used instead of gold leaf for the stars. Once the gold leaf has been applied, work the final embellishments with a fine sable paintbrush.

It will not matter if the final result does not replicate the example illustrated here. What matters, above all, is that the piece should have its own compositional integrity and life.

PER ARDUA AD ASTRA
*The finished piece reflects the meaning of the
words and their relationships. Rhythm
and movement are fundamental
to its success.*

WOOD ENGRAVING

WOOD ENGRAVING FALLS INTO THE same family of print-making methods as woodcuts and linoleum cuts. These are called "relief printing" because a flat surface, destined to receive ink, is cut away into relief. Other methods of transferring ink to paper include squeezing it through a fine mesh, exploiting the adhesive and repellent qualities of a surface, or by using damp paper to extract ink from incised lines into which it has been forced (this is "intaglio" printing).

Of all the printmaking methods, relief printing is the oldest and the simplest method of transferring images to paper. Its history goes back to prints and rubbings made from carved stone by the Chinese in the second century A.D. and to block prints made on fabric some four hundred years before that.

Only in the fourteenth century, however, did relief printing eventually reach Europe. During the fifteenth century it was developed to include printing pictures in color and led to the invention of movable type.

Pictorially, relief prints are identifiable by the cuts appearing as white on the print, whereas in intaglio printing the cuts hold the ink and so appear as black when printed.

Wood engraving is distinguished from other methods of relief printing by its use of fine tools, originally metal engraver's "burins," and the corresponding fine grain of the material engraved, classically boxwood, an innovation attributed to Thomas Bewick in the late eighteenth century. Bewick realized that the white cuts did not merely remove the extraneous matter, but could themselves

create the image. His vast output, and an influential handful of wood engravings by his contemporary William Blake, established the character of these new images. Identical methods are still used today by artists and illustrators.

The wood engraver holds the block with one hand and the tool with the other and turns the block against the tool, usually on a leather sandbag, which raises the block to a convenient height. The tool is a shaped metal rod set in a handle and sharpened to a point. The cross-section of the rod determines the shape of the cutting point, and the four main types of section come in a variety of sizes. The wood block the engraver works on is cut across the grain and must be absolutely flat and smooth to ensure that it will print perfectly. It can be any size (at a cost), but printmakers who

A loose guide is sketched on the block for the engraver to follow but the cuts determine the final image.

THE WOOD ENGRAVING
The image begins to take shape as the background is cut away (above).

want to work on blocks with a dimension larger than about 18 in (46 cm) usually choose a cheaper medium. Most wood engravings are of a modest size. Some contemporary engravers work on synthetic materials such as Perspex, which allows them to work on a larger scale, but the size of the tools and of the cuts remain the determining factors; beyond a certain size, the cuts become too large to blend together sufficiently well and be read as light in the way uniquely characteristic of a wood engraving.

A medium that can reproduce a great deal of detail inspires an intense identification with the emerging image on the

CUTTING THE BLOCK
The block has been lightly inked and the first cuts are made on the edge of the design.

TAKING A PRINT
The finished block is positioned in the press ready for printing.

REVEALING THE IMAGE
Peeling the paper from a block and seeing the print for the first time is an exciting moment.

THE BLOCK AND THE PRINT
Fine adjustments can be carried out once the artist has seen the printed image.

block on the part of the engraver. The fascination of wood engraving lies, not in the physical techniques, but in the artistic vision, the concept, and the draftsmanship. Progress in the art is not made through a mastery of "skills" or of the "craft," but through grasping an understanding of visual language.

Most wood engravers map out the basic shapes of their image on the block before they begin to cut it with engraving tools. A loose outline can be drawn using Indian ink and a steel pen, so as to preserve a springy life in the line. Much can be left undefined, so that the image can take shape while the engraver is cutting. Another approach, however, might be to start from a very exact outline; a third might be to make a complete little tonal painting on the block.

A beginner needs only four or five

tools and an oilstone. An oilstone is essential because the tools must be kept very sharp. Where to begin cutting is also a matter of personal preference and varies greatly. Some artists begin by clearing the edge of the design; others will begin at its heart or at some peripheral point, or systematically with the darkest parts. If you darken the block with a thin film of printing ink, the pen drawing will show through and the white cuts made will be more clearly defined against the surface. Wherever the engraving is begun, work a little at a time, always removing a little curl of wood with the point of the tool, never merely scratching the surface. Hold the tool at an angle that will produce a clean cut. If the angle is too shallow, the tool will skid forward; if it is too steep, it will embed itself in the wood.

Once the image is more or less finished, a print can be taken from the block. Most engravers defer taking a print until the engraving is as complete as possible because printing ink discolors the clean-cut wood, and it is difficult then to judge the effect of the fresh cuts accurately against the stained ones. Inevitably there will always be a number of further adjustments that need to be made before the engraving is ready for final prints to be taken.

Although a printing press is normally used for taking a print from a wood engraving, it is not a necessity. Extremely effective prints can be made by pressing a sheet of paper to an inked block and then burnishing the back of the paper with an old spoon – after all, the whole Japanese printing tradition is built on the hand-burnished print.

LETTERPRESS PRINTING

THE ART OF PRINTING
*Letterpress has been developed and refined
over hundreds of years; the basic processes
have changed very little.*

PRINTING WAS INVENTED BY THE Chinese, who were also the first people to learn how to make paper. Each page of a Chinese book would be printed from a single block of carved wood – a laborious and cumbersome process. In China, as the craft of papermaking developed over the centuries, so did printing; but in Europe the Chinese method remained virtually unchanged until the fifteenth century, when it was revolutionized, in Germany, by Johann Gutenberg (1397-1468).

In his lifetime, Gutenberg, who is believed to have been a goldsmith, saw great advances in smithing and metal-engraving, and applied some of these developments to print. In about 1450 he began experimenting seriously with fruit and oil presses and goldsmithing techniques. His great contributions to

printing were the invention of movable type and a movable bed for the press, so that sheets of paper could easily be drawn in and out of it. The possibility of re-using type, of correcting and altering it after it was set, and of printing faster changed the process decisively; it amounted to a medieval industrial revolution. In fact, it is true to say that the basic principles of book design were established between 1450 and 1525.

Although literacy was still uncommon and printing tightly controlled by law, an enormous variety of printed material – including books, pamphlets, and broadsheets – was produced in this period throughout the western world. The spread of print helped to encourage the development of vernacular literatures and coincided with the decline of Latin as an international language.

Apart from the invention of new letter forms, little changed in the craft of printing until the nineteenth century. Paper continued to be hand-made and was usually printed damp. Type was hand-inked, using sand-filled leather pads. It was the cast-iron, steam-driven presses, in use by the 1820s, that brought full mechanization to printing. As a medium, the press became much freer, if only because it was impossible to control; and increased literacy created the first mass market for print.

Until the 1880s type was still cast by hand, but the Linotype and Monotype machines, invented toward the end of the century, brought almost total mechanization. Hand printing has survived in small private presses which have conserved many of the skills of design as well as techniques that have been

TRAYS OF TYPE

Complete sets of type are stored in special cases ready for use.

SETTING THE TEXT

The compositor arranges each piece of type in a composing stick.

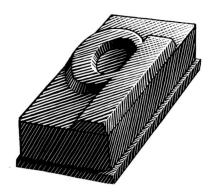

A PIECE OF TYPE

The relief image of a letter is cut in reverse so that when printed on a sheet of paper it reads correctly.

lost in industry. Recent developments in computerized type-setting have been technically advanced, but they remain aesthetically unsophisticated.

Nevertheless, printing is one of the few crafts in which relations between mechanized and craft branches are often cordial. Private-press books may be taken up by commerical publishers, or used as pilots for larger projects. Private presses – including one-person businesses – continue to flourish, producing everything from letterheads to complex illustrated books.

The technique of setting a single line of type is the basic skill of letterpress printing. Once one line is set, others can be added and a full-page broadsheet can be printed. To make a book, the process is extended but not essentially changed. A sheet of printed paper

with two panels of type can be folded to make a leaflet; if the back of the sheet is printed, too, it becomes a four-page booklet. Simple bindings made of stitched board, and illustrations in the form of wood block engravings can be incorporated to make small books. Line drawings can be converted photomechanically into relief blocks or "cuts."

The letterhead shown on page 97 is printed on a small proof press. The other equipment used is a composing stick; "furniture," the metal or plastic bars that hold the type in place; a type tray with at least 80 divisions; a "chase," or frame, to hold the set type; "quoins" (wedges) and a "quoin key" (or a screwdriver) to keep the chase rigid; ink and type. Two type sizes are used, and a complete set of each should be obtained. These will include upper and lower case

THE TYPESETTER'S SKILL
*Great attention is paid to the spacing between
letters and words when preparing type.*

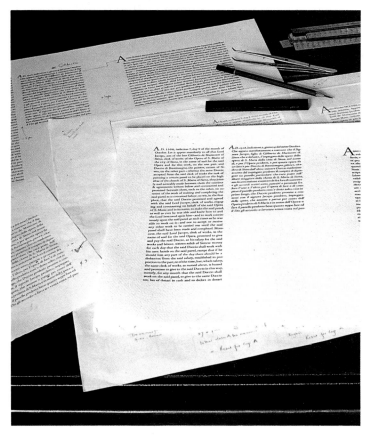

PAGE PROOFS
*The first prints for a book usually require a
number of corrections.*

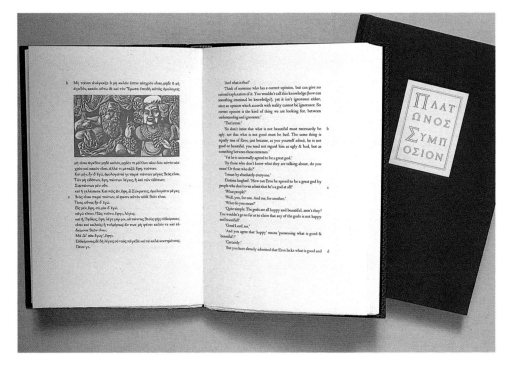

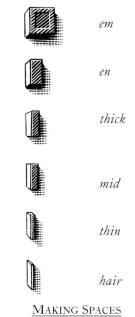

em

en

thick

mid

thin

hair

MAKING SPACES
*Various sizes of non-printing material
(above) ensure a page looks balanced.*

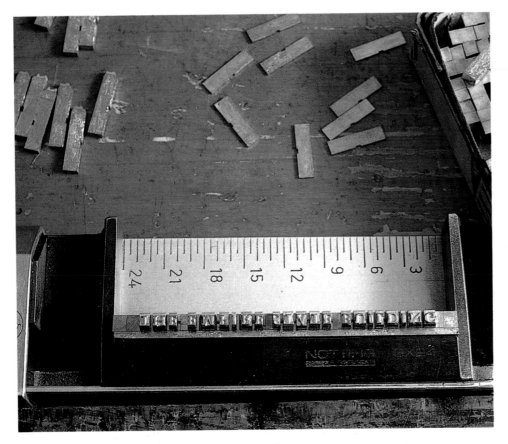

PREPARING THE LETTERHEAD
*The composing stick is set to a certain length
and the type spaced across it.*

POSITIONING THE PAPER
*A number of sheets are accurately positioned
on the printing press.*

(capital and small letter) alphabets, figures, and punctuation marks, all in roman and italic type-faces. There will also be non-printing pieces of type used for spacing. In every size of type the spacing system is identical. There are five distinct sizes: ems, ens, thicks, mids, and thins. A hair space is also used for very fine adjustments of space and can be slightly variable. All of these should be kept in separate compartments in the tray. Subdividers are often added to the original divisions of the type tray.

Once the wording and design have been decided, the next step is to select the appropriate type sizes. Set the line

LOCKED IN POSITION
*The composition is locked into a chase and is
ready to be fixed into the press.*

TAKING A PRINT
*The success of the print relies on even pressure
when transferring the ink to the paper.*

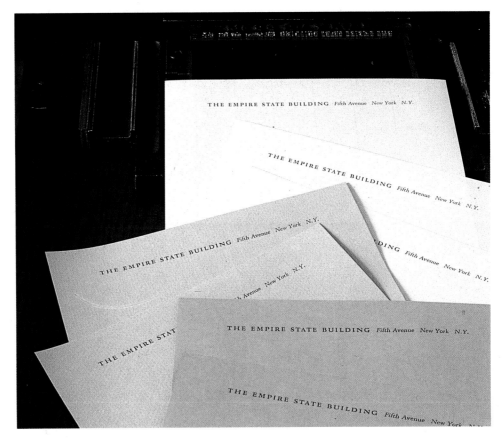

THE LETTERHEAD
*Making your own, personal, headed paper is
an extremely satisfying first project.*

length on the composing stick; insert a piece of furniture of the same length into the angle of the stick; and lock it into position. Select the type from the tray, and insert it in the stick in the correct order, reading right to left, but with the characters upside down.

The non-printing pieces of type are used to fill the length of the line. Exact, even spacing is one of the hallmarks of high-quality printing. The individual letters must then be pressed flat and the type "locked up" in the chase, where it is held rigid with furniture. Tighten the quoins with the quoin key or screwdriver, to make the block rigid.

The next step is to ink up the type. The amount of ink used depends upon the quantity of type to be printed. For a letterhead, only a small amount is needed. It is dabbed onto the ink roller,

and another, distributing roller spreads it evenly. Position the paper with grippers, adjusting it to ensure that the edges of the paper are parallel with the type. An experienced printer will make many delicate alterations at this stage. The paper should be backed with several other sheets to give the necessary pressure. Place the type on the printing bed, and wind the press along the cogged carriageway on either side of the bed.

Up to 200 sheets an hour can be printed in this way. They can be left in heaps to dry; however, no more than 25 sheets should be stacked together, in order to prevent smudging.

CATEGORIES OF TYPE-FACE
*The wide variety of type-faces are based on
either serif or sans serif (right).*

BOOKBINDING

TOOLS AND EQUIPMENT
*A bookbinder employs tools that have been
developed to be perfect for their task.*

THE USE OF BINDINGS CAN BE traced back to AD 200 when the written word moved from scrolls to folded, flat papyrus and parchment sheets. Astonishingly, these relatively crude bindings were sewn in a manner comparable to the machine-bound books of today. The first time bound books appeared in Europe was probably in the seventh century, but it was not until the advent of printing using movable type, in the fifteenth century, that large-scale production of books began.

In recent years, a small number of individual designer-bookbinders, working in the tradition of artist-craftsmen such as William Morris and twentieth-century French binders such as Pierre Legrain, have sought to uphold the best traditions of the craft and introduce innovatory designs and techniques.

To make a paper-bound book measuring 7 x 3¼ in (18 x 8.5 cm), the following materials and equipment are required: six sheets of medium-weight drawing paper each cut to measure 12½ x 14¼ in (32 x 36 cm), one sheet of hand-made, heavy-weight paper 10½ in (27 cm) square, a strip of vellum, a strip of decorative paper (optional), P.V.A. adhesive, a spool of linen or carpet thread, a sharp knife, an x-acto knife, a pin, a steel ruler, a bone folder or soft-pointed letter opener, a right-angled triangle, a T-square, a needle, and a small pair of pliers.

The finished book has 48 plain pages. These are made from six folded sections of eight pages each, each section made from a sheet of the medium-weight paper. To make a section, fold one sheet of paper in half, bringing the two short

edges together. Slit through the fold with a sharp knife. Turn the paper 90 degrees to the right, fold in half again and slit. For the third fold do not turn the paper, but bring the two long edges together. Do not slit. Make another five sections in the same way.

Next, take the sheet of heavy-weight paper to make the cover. Each edge of the cover will have a turn-in approximately one quarter of the depth of the finished book. Mark the depth of the top turn-in (approximately 1¾ in [4.5 cm]) with a pinprick, and score along the edge of a ruler at this point on the wrong side of the paper with the bone folder or letter opener. Fold over the turn-in with the bone folder. Crease down the fold along the score line and rub along the edge of the fold, covering it with a piece of paper to avoid making it shine.

Measure the height of the page sections against the cover and add ⅛ in
(4 mm) to give a 1/16 in (2 mm) overlap at
the head and tail of the book. Mark the
score line for the tail turn-in, and crease
as before. With the x-acto knife, trim
the turn-ins to match.

Next, make the two folds that form
the spine of the book. Find the middle of
the inside of the cover. Make two pinpricks to left and right of the center of
the paper so that the pinpricks are ⅜ in
(1 cm) apart. Using a right-angled triangle, score down the cover at these
points, and fold over each side. Turn the
cover over, and score a line 1/16 in (2 mm)

DIFFERENT TYPES OF BINDING
Hardcovered bindings are considerably more
complex than paper ones.

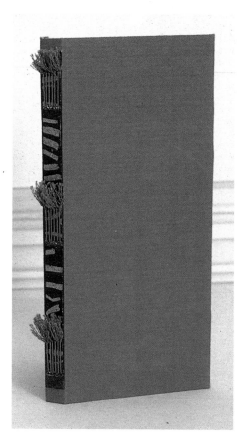

THE PAPERBOUND BOOK
*As a final decorative touch the stitching
threads have been frayed.*

BASIC INGREDIENTS
*For a perfectly finished binding, make sure to
use the right paper and equipment.*

outside each spine fold to ease flexibility.

To make the fore edge (side) turn-ins, place the fold of one of the six paper sections on the right-hand spine fold of the cover. Measure ¼ in (5 mm) beyond the edge of the paper section, and mark with a pinprick. Score at this point with the bone folder against the edge of the triangle and fold up. With the x-acto knife, trim the turn-in to the same size as the other turn-ins. Repeat this procedure to make the left-hand turn-in.

Next, cut the corners of the book. Open out the fore edge turn-ins. Start at the bottom right-hand corner of the cover. On the bottom edge, mark a point ⅛ in (4 mm) out from the fore edge fold line. Draw a line from this point to the top right-hand corner of this turn-in to form a triangle. Cut through both layers of paper along this line. Cut

the remaining corners in the same way and refold the fore edge turn-ins. Trim the loose, underlying flap so that it does not jut out. Crease down the corners with the bone folder.

Since no adhesive is used for this book (except for attaching the optional spine decoration), the corners are secured by making a "yapp" edge. Score a line ⅛ in (4 mm) in from the inside of each fore edge, and fold up carefully so that it stands up at 90 degrees.

The spine of the cover is strengthened with a back strip of vellum, which can be left plain or covered with decorative paper. With an x-acto knife, cut the strip so that it is minutely shorter and narrower than the spine.

The next stage is to sew the folded paper sections, the cover, and the back strip together along the spine. The holes

for sewing must be in pairs, but how many there are or where they are positioned is each maker's choice. Make a paper stitch guide, using a piece of paper exactly the same length as the spine. Mark along the edge of the paper evenly-spaced pairs of stitching holes. This stitch guide can be used for marking the folded paper sections, the spine, and the back strip.

First, take the six paper sections. Align them carefully, one on top of the other, at the table's edge, and put a weight on them to stop them moving. Use the stitch guide to transfer the marks to the fold of the top section. Continue these marks down the rest of the sections with a pencil line, using a T-square for accuracy. Then mark the points on the inside of the spine and back strip with a pencil, and draw pencil lines

MAKING A BINDING
At every stage of the cutting, folding, and stitching, accuracy is imperative.

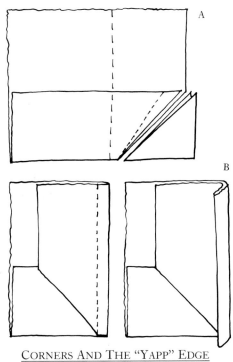

A

B

CORNERS AND THE "YAPP" EDGE
Cut each corner as indicated (a). Fold up the fore edges at a right angle (b).

across them. Make six pencil dots equidistant across each of these lines to indicate where each section will be stitched. With the needle, prick through all these marks on the folded sections, the spine, and the back strip.

Use the linen or carpet thread to sew the book together. If it is difficult to pull the needle through the thickness of paper, use small pliers to help. Start at the first hole at one end of the book. From the outside, push the needle through the back strip, spine, and an open paper section, to the inside. Then push the needle back through the next paired hole through all the layers to the outside. Knot the thread together and pull tight. Cut the ends of the threads leaving a short tail. Repeat this procedure for the following pairs of holes and the remaining paper sections.

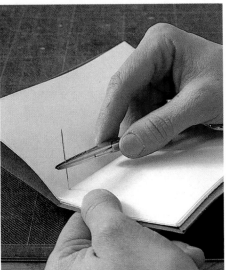

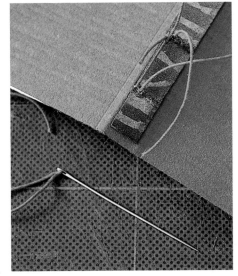

PAPIER MÂCHÉ

FREE-STANDING PAPER SCULPTURES
*The artist draws inspiration from many
sources, including Mexican art, for these
papier mâché figures and icons.*

T HE FRENCH TERM "PAPIER
mâché" means literally, "chewed
paper." It is a highly versatile, creative
medium whose history is probably as old
as paper itself.

Papier mâché objects, traditionally,
are made by one of two methods: lam-
inating involves building up layers of
glue-soaked paper, usually newspaper;
whereas pulping requires the paper to be
boiled, mashed to a pulp, and mixed
with glue. The resulting substance can
be used to form shapes in much the same
way as clay. Both methods have been
widely used in many cultures. The
earliest-known examples of papier
mâché are lacquered war helmets and
pot lids made in China around AD 200.

In eighteenth- and nineteenth-
century Europe there were papier
mâché factories making architectural

ornaments, bric-à-brac, and even furniture. Paper pulp was mashed in large
vats using steam power; the pulp was
either pressed into sheets, which could
then be steam-pressed to fabricate other
items, or poured into molds. George
Washington ordered papier mâché ceiling ornaments, made by an English
firm, to adorn his residence.

Notable examples from Germany include snuffboxes produced in the 1760s
at a factory in Brunswick. In the 1880s a
Dresden watch-maker produced a time-
piece made entirely of paper. Papier
mâché boards were used to make parti-
tions on ocean liners, and, in the 1790s,
they were even used to build a church in
Norway which lasted over 30 years.
Such applications testify to the surprising durability of the medium.

In the twentieth century, papier

mâché has been most commonly
employed as a cheap, if somewhat
messy, craft material for children. But
in recent years a number of professional
artists have recognized its potential, and
have taken up the craft.

Because it is malleable, inexpensive,
and requires no complex techniques,
papier mâché is regarded as an unre-
strained, wide-ranging medium. It can
be controlled to meet the needs of design
and self-expression. Artists, frustrated
by the inflexibility of other media, have
turned to papier mâché to produce im-
mediate, vigorous work.

The work shown here uses a laminate
technique to produce a variety of objects
ranging from relief-sculptures to usable
objects including dolls, doll house furniture, and mirrors. A casting technique has been developed by the artist

A PAIR OF JOINTED DOLLS
*These highly individual figures (left) appeal
to adults and children alike.*

SHAPING THE BODY
*Take particular care when shaping the
modeling clay for the body and limbs.*

LAYERS OF PAPER
*Two different-colored papers are used to build
up six perfectly smooth layers.*

EMPTY SHELLS
*The arms, legs and body are left to dry and
then cut from the modeling clay with a knife.*

which allows more control over the forms. The foundation is made of modeling clay, over which layers of paper are applied. The pulping method is used in small quantities to model areas of relief in some places.

The work is highly finished with gesso and acrylic paints. From a distance it can be mistaken for clay or wood. One of the attributes of papier mâché is that it can pose as something else, while being instantly indentifiable, because of its lightness, if it is picked up.

Papier mâché has always been a popular folk art medium, notably in South America and India. The papier mâché dolls shown here are inspired by traditional, jointed, paper dolls which are still made in Mexico; they are made using the layering method on a modeled form. To make a doll the following mat-erials and equipment are needed: modeling clay, mold-makers' soft soap, newspaper (two different colors, if possible), a large bowl, cellulose cold-water paste (wallpaper paste), plastic-based water-proof glue, an x-acto knife, gesso (preferably acrylic), vibrant acrylic paints in a range of colors, matte acrylic varnish, black hat elastic, a mattress needle, and masking tape.

Each part of the doll must be hand-molded in modeling clay: torso and head in one piece, a left and a right arm, and a left and a right leg. The doll may be made to any size, but the smaller the doll the more durable it will be. Whatever size is chosen it is important to keep the parts of the body in proportion. The measurements for the two dolls shown here are: head and torso, 6¼ in (16 cm) long; arms, 3½ in (9 cm) long and ⅜ in (1 cm) in diameter; legs, 4¾ in (12 cm) long, ¾ in (2 cm) in diameter. To make it easier to remove the paper after drying, it is advisable to cover the model with a layer of mold-makers' soft soap before applying the paper.

The next stage is to cover each of the parts with six layers of newspaper and paste. Tear or cut the newspaper into 2 in (5 cm) squares, and prepare the water-based paste according to the manufacturer's instructions, in a large bowl. Using your hands, smear the paste evenly on both sides of the newspaper squares; tear each piece into smaller strips, ⅜ in (1 cm) wide. Apply these strips to the clay models until the whole surface is covered. Take care when applying each strip to smooth out air bubbles. Repeat this process until six layers have been applied. In order to

PAINTING AND ASSEMBLING
*When all the sections of the doll are complete,
they can be joined with black elastic.*

keep track of the layers it is helpful to use two different-colored newspapers; used alternately, it will be possible to see when a layer is complete.

Allow the parts to dry thoroughly; this can be done by leaving them in a warm room overnight. When the parts are dry, cut them from the clay, using the x-acto knife, in two equal parts, somewhat like an Easter egg.

Glue the parts together again, using the plastic-based waterproof glue. Hold the two halves in place with strips of masking tape; this will ensure that they are joined accurately.

When the glue is dry, remove the masking tape, and apply another layer of paper over the seam, as before, to create a completely smooth surface.

Paint each piece with at least four coats of gesso. If acrylic is used, all four

coats can be done in one day, since it dries very quickly. It is important to take care with this stage; a well-prepared surface will take the paint easily and give the piece a highly-finished appearance.

The pieces of the doll are painted before being assembled. It is helpful to consider the doll as a whole by laying out the pieces in their natural configuration. The doll can be painted in any way; but the style lends itself to vibrant color combinations such as the pinks, oranges, blues, and yellows used here. It is perhaps most effective to paint a single-colored ground, then to select a strong contrast for a pattern; socks, shoes and hair are most effective in black and white. Check that the pattern on each part relates to the whole. When the paint is dry, give each part one coat of matte acrylic varnish. Join the limbs to

the torso with black hat elastic, threaded onto a mattress needle long enough to join the parts in one movement. Push the threaded needle from one outer thigh through the hips to the other outer thigh. Secure the elastic at each end with a single knot. Repeat this process with the arms: from one outer arm through the chest to the other outer arm. The elastic should be knotted tightly enough to keep the limbs in place, but it must also allow free movement.

The doll is durable enough to be played with, but would not be suitable for very young children unless non-toxic paints and varnish are used.

A FEAST OF COLOR
*Bright colors and the occasional touch of gold
make these sculptures visually exciting.*

KITCHEN CRAFTS

GOAT CHEESE □ FESTIVAL BREAD □ COOKIE MAKING

SMOKING FISH □ CHOCOLATE MAKING □ PRESERVES

CIDER MAKING □ BASKETRY □ DRIED FLOWERS

CANDLE MAKING

GOAT CHEESE

IRRESISTIBLE DELIGHTS
*A selection of creamy goat cheese (right)
rolled in herbs, decorated, or wrapped in
leaves, is almost too good to eat.*

THE FRENCH ARE FAMOUS FOR their cheeses – and, in particular, for their goat cheese, or *chèvre*. A display of these delicacies in a good *fromagerie* looks more like an array of pastries and desserts than cheeses. There is *Banon* from Provence, a festive-looking cheese, with its sweet-chestnut leaf wrapping and tie. There are other kinds coated in charcoal and salt: the circular *Selles-sur-Cher*, a sweet, nutty cheese from central France, with a blue-black surface, white cheese and smooth texture; *Graçay*, a truncated cone which has a mild goaty smell and medium-strong flavor; and *Valençay*, a sawn-off pyramid which is dusted with wood ash and has a delicate flavor. *Sainte-Maure* is easily recognizable by the stick of straw poking out either end. It is made in Touraine, "the Garden of France."

Crottins de Chavignol with its moldy appearance is perhaps the most intimidating; it is a dry, tough cheese with a sharp, pungent tang. Its name is not very encouraging either, for it means horse-droppings, but the cheese is revered in French cuisine. Variations of these French cheeses are made in other European countries. And even in countries, like the United States, where goat cheese is not produced in any quantity, the growing popularity of imported goat cheese is evident on the cheese counters of the better delicatessens.

Goats are believed to have originated in the East; the earliest records of them come from Persia. In Europe they were considered valuable domestic animals; easy to feed and keep, and an invaluable source of meat and milk. Gradually, however, cattle and sheep ousted the

FRESH GOAT'S MILK

It is possible to buy goat's milk if you don't
have your own supply.

HANGING TO DRAIN

The curds are wrapped in cheesecloth and left
to drip overnight.

THE NECESSARY EQUIPMENT

Using simple kitchen items goat cheese can
quite easily be made at home.

goat from its dominant role in husbandry. Even so, herds of goats are still kept in many parts of the world, and because they will thrive almost anywhere and live on almost nothing they continue to be a favorite possession of peasants and nomads.

Ironically, this "poor man's cow," as it is sometimes called, is the source of some of the most expensive cheeses. The character of the cheese changes with keeping and the season, being fragrant in spring and summer and more acid as the herbage dies back in the autumn. Goat's milk contains fewer bacteria than cow's milk, and, in principle, does not need pasteurizing (a heat treatment that partially sterilizes the milk), allowing seasonal variations and a fuller flavor to pervade the cheese. Goats have a short lactating period, so the milk, and there-

fore the cheese, is periodic. A productive nanny goat will give over one gallon (3.8 liters) of milk a day at her peak, but she can be notoriously capricious.

Farmhouse goat cheese thus varies considerably from one region to another. The same cheese will also vary with age. Fresh, they can look rather innocuous, but they usually tend to be slightly sour, with a mild peppery sting. This deepens as the cheese matures, but if left too long it acidifies and the cheese develops an overpowering, eye-watering, billy-goat flavor. French connoisseurs prefer the aged *chèvres*.

To make goat cheese at home, either buy goat's milk, or take milk from your own goats. Most of the equipment that is required can be found in the kitchen; if not, it is easily obtainable from a hardware store. A double-boiler is ideal for

READ FOR THE FLAVORING
*When the curds split cleanly, salt and herbs
or garlic can be added.*

WEIGHING AND MOLDING
*The cheeses are formed into small white
rounds and weighed for packing.*

making cheese, but a large saucepan will do, provided care is taken that the milk does not burn or stick to the bottom. A glass or stainless steel measuring pitcher that is easy to clean, a thermometer, a ladle (preferably a perforated one), a square of cheesecloth, a colander, and string will also be needed.

There are two special ingredients: a "starter," which ripens the milk and promotes the necessary lactic acids essential for cheesemaking, and rennet, a coagulant. Cheese rennet is quite easy to obtain; try your local health food store. In some areas, however, it can be difficult to find the starter; an alternative is to use cultured buttermilk, which is widely available and gives good results. A starter is not absolutely vital, but cheese made without it, especially if made from pasteurized milk, will be ex-

tremely bland. Other ingredients are salt and fresh herbs, such as thyme, rosemary, chives, and parsley or garlic.

The simplest recipe to start off with is a soft, goat's-milk cheese. It is critical to maintain the room temperature between 65 and 70°F (18 and 21°C); if it is only slightly cooler, the curds and whey will take longer to separate, but if it is much too cold or too hot, the action of the rennet will be completely inhibited.

Start by making a small quantity. Heat 2½ pints (1.18 liters) of goat's milk to 90°F (32°C) and stir in the starter; after half an hour add 14 drops of rennet. Make sure that the milk is still warm, 75°F (24°C), and leave it to coagulate, which should take roughly 12 hours. The curds are ready when they split cleanly as a finger is pushed through them. Line the colander with a

STRAINING THE CURDS
*At home, a kitchen colander, a perforated
ladle, and a square of cheesecloth are
sufficient for this process.*

CHESTNUT-LEAF WRAPPING
The cheese is rolled and wrapped in brandy-soaked sweet-chestnut leaves.

FRESHLY CRUSHED PEPPERCORNS
A black-peppercorn coating enhances the flavor of the cheese.

HERBS FOR CHEESES
Chopped chives, parsley, rosemary, and garlic can all be added to the cheese.

square of clean cheesecloth, and ladle the junket-like mass onto the fabric. Draw up the corners, tie them in a knot and suspend the curds where they can be left to drip overnight. The following morning take them down and mix in some salt to taste and some fresh herbs; or save the herbs to coat the outside. Mold the cheese into a round, or use "Scotch hands" (wooden butter pats) to form oblongs which you can then decorate with currant or oak leaves, or herbs.

When making cheese it is important to be methodical and scrupulously clean; sterilize all equipment between batches. Different results will be achieved from day to day, but do not give up after a couple of experiments. The same recipe given to six people would produce half a dozen different cheeses; the art lies with the cheesemaker.

The cheese should be eaten fresh, within one or two days of being made. However, if the cheese is cured in spirits and wrapped in leaves, the crust will be sterilized, and the cheese will last a little longer. A *Banon* could be made, similar to the one shown (above left); in this case, sweet-chestnut leaves were steeped in brandy until they turned an olive green, and then wrapped around the cheeses and secured with raffia; when the parcels are opened the curds are mottled with brown veins from the tannin in the leaves. As an alternative, the cheese could be dusted with charcoal like the French *Selles-sur-Cher*; to obtain the charcoal, finely grind the residue from a barbecue. Whatever coating is chosen the cheese will remain tender and at its best for only about ten days; it will then start to turn acidic.

A Seasonal Flavor
The flavor of goat cheese is extremely variable; often mild but sometimes pungently strong.

A Charcoal Dusting
Finely grind the residue from a barbecue for this unusual, and quite edible, finish.

FESTIVAL BREAD

THE BAKER'S MASTERPIECE
The wheatsheaf loaf (left) is one way by which a baker can demonstrate his expertise and love of baking.

FESTIVAL BREADS HAVE BEEN MADE for centuries to celebrate abundant harvests. At first, the shapes of these loaves must have been quite simple – probably two circles of dough one on top of the other, rather like a large, flat brioche. As Western cultures became more complex the designs became more intricate. They developed as important symbols of plenty and became a focal point at the Christian harvest thanksgiving service – a long-established European tradition which inspired the Pilgrims' Thanksgiving feast.

The design of the loaf was determined by the nature of the community. The wheatsheaf form – most commonly thought of as the harvest loaf – originated in arable farming communities. Where fruit was the main crop, the loaf would be a low-relief plaque in the form

A HARVEST PLATTER
Bakers in coastal areas often use the Biblical account of the feeding of the five thousand, as a theme for a decorative loaf at harvest festivals.

of a cornucopia or a basket overflowing with fruit. On the coast, the festival loaf was usually an oval plaque depicting the Christian image of the five loaves and two fishes. These more decorative loaves are known to have been made for at least six hundred years.

The loaves were not intended to be eaten, though they may have been symbolically broken in church. These festival breads served – and still serve – another purpose. They allowed the baker to develop and show off his skills; it was considered to be his virtuoso performance. In early times the baker was considered one of the foremost craftsmen in the community; bakers would stamp their mark on their loaves in the way a potter marks his work or a painter signs a picture. Examples of these marks were found on bread preserved in the

KNEADING THE DOUGH
*Use a heavy-duty mixer (right) or a strong
pair of hands to knead the dough.*

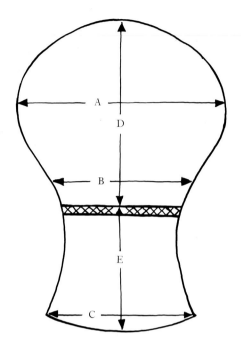

THE WHEATSHEAF TEMPLATE
*A = 9 in (22 cm); B = 6¼ in (16 cm);
C = 6 in (15 cm); D = 7½ in (19 cm);
E = 4½ in (11 cm).*

lava at Pompeii.

Today the festival loaf is still made in
some communities for traditional Christian harvest thanksgiving. But it is also
used by bakers to demonstrate their
expertise to customers. A master baker
may use a varnished harvest loaf as window display all year round. Most bakers
have the skills and knowledge required
to make festival loaves, and enjoy the
challenge of making them but the
demand for festival loaves is now slight.

A wheatsheaf loaf, based on a scaleddown version of the master baker's design and using a traditional recipe, can
be made in a domestic oven. The dough
used can be formed into any shape, so
the potential for making decorative
loaves is limitless. Food coloring can be
used to enhance the design.

It is important to allow plenty of time

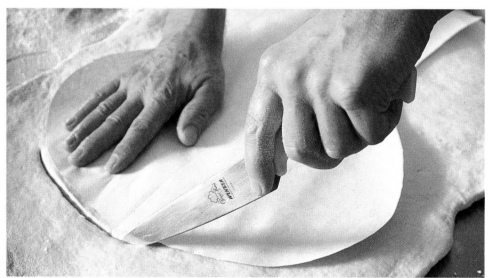

CUTTING THE BASIC SHAPE
*Lay the template over the rolled out dough
and cut accurately around it at an angle.*

REMOVING THE EXCESS DOUGH
*If the surface has been well-floured the dough
will come away easily (left).*

<u>DOCKING THE BASE FOR BAKING</u>
*Using a baking "docker," or a fork or
skewer, prick the entire surface of the base.*

– about four hours – to make a wheat-sheaf loaf. The dough performs best if it is kept cool and moist while being worked, and handling must be slow and very careful.

To make the wheatsheaf loaf the following ingredients are required: 12½ cups, or 3⅛ lb, (1.4 kg) of medium-strength white bread flour, 4 teaspoons (25 g) salt, scant 2 tablespoons (25 g) fat (preferably lard), scant ¼ cup (25 g) powdered milk, 1 rounded teaspoon (5 g) dried yeast, 1⅝ pints (750 ml) cold water, and 2 beaten eggs. The following equipment is needed: a large mixing bowl, a pitcher, a kitchen knife, a fork or skewer, a rolling pin, and a cookie sheet. Paper, pencil, and scissors are needed to make the template.

The ingredients given will form a very tight, strong dough and, therefore,

the use of an electric mixer is not recommended, unless the machine is heavy-duty. The dough must be very thoroughly mixed until it forms a taut ball, and this is best achieved by hand.

To make the dough, first combine all the ingredients except the yeast, water, and eggs. Dissolve the yeast in the water, make a well in the flour mixture, and pour in the yeast-water. Now knead the dough, until it is smooth and pliable; this may take as long as 10 minutes. It is better to knead the dough too much rather than too little.

The dough must then be left to relax, wrapped in a plastic bag, for at least 30 minutes but preferably for an hour. It will not rise much because of the low yeast content.

To form the dough into a wheatsheaf shape, first draw a template. The dimen-

sions of the wheatsheaf using this quantity of dough are: 12 in (30 cm) long, 9 in (22 cm) wide at the widest part of the head of wheat and 6 in (15 cm) wide at the foot of the stalks. Fold a rectangular piece of paper in half. Divide the width measurements of the wheatsheaf in half to allow for the double thickness of paper. Mark the edge of the base, the waist, and the widest point of the head with a pencil. Then join these points with curved lines on one side of the paper to form one half of the wheatsheaf. Cut along the lines and open out the folded paper for the full template. Trim to form smooth curves.

Roll out all of the dough into a rectangular shape, just larger than the template. The base of the wheatsheaf should be slightly raised in the center, sloping gently to the edges to give a domed

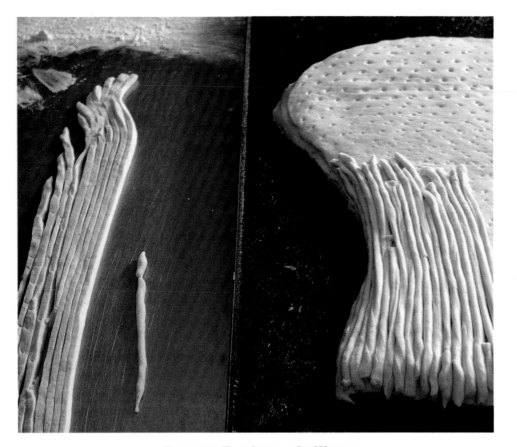

FORMING THE STALKS OF WHEAT
*Lay thin, rolled strips of dough randomly
over the base of the wheatsheaf.*

THE WAIST TIE
*Braid three thin strips of dough together
to form a tie.*

A HARVEST MOUSE
*With a small piece of dough, make a little
mouse to sit at the center of the waist tie. Use
black peppercorns for the eyes, and make two
ears and a tail.*

effect. Place the template on the dough and cut around it at a 45 degree angle to prevent shrinkage. If the dough is cut straight, it will turn under when baked. Keep the remaining dough, which will be used for the wheat and for decoration, wrapped in a plastic bag to prevent it from forming a skin.

Place the base on a clean, lightly greased cookie sheet. Brush the dough with water to prevent a skin from forming; if this happens the surface of the loaf will crack in the oven. The dough must be well "docked," the baker's term for aerating (the same principle as in pricking a piecrust). The professional baker uses a spiked roller called a docker, but the same results can be achieved using a fork or skewer.

The next stage is to form thin strands of dough about ¼ in (5 mm) in diameter and about 7 in (18 cm) long to represent the stalks of wheat. These are laid on the base, not uniformly but in a way that suggests a sheaf; some may be broken in half or slightly overlapping.

To make the wheat ears, take thicker strands of dough, approximately ½ in (1 cm) in diameter and any convenient length. Place a strand of dough on the table, and make diagonal cuts ¼ in (5 mm) in length into it at regular intervals, working from top to bottom. Roll the strand over slightly and repeat the process. Roll once more and repeat again. Thus the strip of dough has been cut into on three "sides." Now cut the strip into shorter pieces, about 1 in (2.5 cm) long. Repeat this until you have made enough ears of wheat to cover the head of the wheatsheaf plentifully.

Place the ears of wheat on the head,

120

EARS OF WHEAT
*Strips of dough and a pair of scissors are all
that is needed to make simple ears of wheat.*

building up the pattern from the outside inward and from the bottom working upward. The ears should overlap slightly and be placed randomly.

For the ties, make a three-strand braid, using strands ¼ in (5 mm) in diameter and 16 in (40 cm) long and cut it in half. Tuck one end of each piece under the edge of the loaf at the waist. Bring the braids together in the middle and overlap them as shown.

Finally, glaze the whole of the wheat-sheaf twice with an egg wash to heighten the color of the finished loaf. Brush the surface thoroughly with the egg, leave it to stand for 10 minutes, then brush thoroughly again.

The dough must now be allowed to relax, or "prove," for 30 minutes at room temperature in a draft-free place. Wrap the loaf in plastic to maintain moisture. Do not allow a skin to form.

Bake the loaf in a moderate oven 400°F (200°C) for one hour. It must be allowed to bake slowly to avoid rapid expansion. Check from time to time that the loaf is not browning too quickly; if it is, turn the oven down.

When the loaf has achieved the full wheatsheaf shape and color, remove it from the oven and allow it to cool.

A harvest platter can be made using half the amount of dough. Roll out a circle of dough measuring 10 in (25 cm), prick it with a fork and lay it on a greased cookie sheet. Brush with water. Shape five loaves and two fishes and attach them to the base. Make a three-strand braid to decorate the outside of the platter. Leave to prove and bake at the same temperature as the wheatsheaf loaf for 40 minutes.

HARVEST FESTIVAL
*Pride of place is often given to the wheatsheaf
loaf at traditional harvest celebrations.*

COOKIE MAKING

METAL CUTTERS

The dough can be cut with a simple scalloped edge, or in novelty shapes.

BAKING IN QUANTITY

Racks of cookies are carefully monitored to ensure perfect results.

STACKED FOR DREDGING

Cookies are left to cool, then sprinkled with fine granulated sugar.

MAKING COOKIES IS PART OF THE repertoire of any small local bakery and all over North America and Europe there are regional specialties. The basic ingredients – flour, fat, eggs, milk, and sugar – can be varied with the addition of spices, fruit, or nuts. In a typical English family bakery, six to eight varieties of cookie (or "biscuits," as they are called in Britain) may be made weekly.

Pastries and cookies have long been associated with religious customs; for example, they are eaten at the Christian festivals of Christmas and Easter; and, in Central Europe, St Valentine's Day is celebrated with gaily-colored frosted cookies. In Victorian England, children were given bundles of sugared ladyfingers, tied with a black ribbon, to carry and consume during funerals. The recipe given here is a specialty of England's West Country, baked – as the name indicates – at Easter.

Cookies fall broadly into several main types, including the crunchy type, chewy varieties, and the smooth, flat shortbread type. This bakery's crunchy cookies are made from a soft, sticky cookie "batter" which is placed on cookie sheets in small irregular mounds. The finished cookie is puffy, yet rugged and crumbly. Shortbreads, usually have a higher proportion of butter to flour than crunchy cookies, and Easter Cookies have a small amount of egg added. The shortbread dough has a dry, crumbly consistency similar to piecrust. It is rolled out and cut into shapes.

In a bakery the cookie mixture is usually made in a large cake-mixer. Mixture that is to be cut into shapes is then pressed into a thin sheet by three rollers. This sheet is transferred to a belt which has been automatically dusted with flour and then passes under a rotary cutter which cuts scalloped-edge disks. The uncooked cookies are picked off the belt by hand and placed on trays. The trays are stacked on racks, each of which may hold a thousand cookies or more. When the ovens have reached the correct temperature, the racks are wheeled in and placed on turntables, which rotate in the hot air as the cookies bake. The cookies are then cooled in a draft of fresh air and packed the same day.

Cookie baking is highly skilled; close observation is required at all stages of mixing, cutting or forming, and baking. The dough must look and feel right so that it will take a shape and bake to the correct firmness and color.

EASTER COOKIES

16 tablespoons, or ½ lb (225 g) butter
3 cups (450 g) all-purpose white flour
1 tablespoon whole milk
1 medium egg, beaten
1⅛ cup (225 g) fine granulated sugar
zest of half a lemon
pinch each of nutmeg, cinnamon, cloves, and allspice
minute pinch of baking powder
¼ cup (30 g) currants
fine granulated sugar for dusting

Cube and soften the butter then blend it with one-third of the flour. Add the remaining flour, and mix. Work in the milk, egg, sugar, zest of lemon, and spices. Finally add the baking powder dispersed in a little milk, mix again and lightly fold in the currants. Roll out the dough to a thickness of ¼ in (5 mm). Cut it into large disks with a cookie-cutter, and bake on a greased and floured cookie sheet at 425°F (220°C) for 12 to 14 minutes. Cool on a wire rack and sprinkle with the sugar.

When making cookies for the first time, remember that they do not crisp up until cool and that overcooking will produce an unpalatable result. Texture and color are just as important as flavor when making cookies. Domestic oven temperatures vary considerably and it is worth testing cookie recipes a couple of times, noting the temperatures, to arrive at the best possible combination of crispness and color.

A very little lemon juice or lemon essence could be added to this recipe for Easter Cookies. Experiment with decorative wooden "prints," and metal cookie cutters in different shapes.

JUST-BAKED EASTER COOKIES
The appeal lies not just in the taste, but in the texture and color.

SMOKING FISH

A PAIR OF BRICK OVENS
*Prepared fish are placed on racks and
suspended in a light smoke (left).*

THE TASTE AND APPEARANCE OF food depends upon how it is preserved, as well as how it is cooked. And the way food looks influences our expectations about its taste – which is why so many manufacturers today add artificial color to food.

With growing concern about chemical preservatives and coloring, there is renewed interest in natural methods of preserving food, such as salting, pickling, and smoking. These are processes that kill, or help to kill, the bacteria that make food rot. They are themselves chemical processes but have been proven over the centuries to be relatively safe, as well as tasty and environmentally kind.

Salting, smoking, and pickling, especially of fish (although eggs, cheese and meat are also smoked), go back

several thousand years. Many of the ancient civilizations, from China to Greece, and Rome to Byzantium, were skilled at preserving foods. Salting and smoking were the most widespread, especially in cultures that depended heavily on fish – which include the North American Indians, the Vikings, and the Celts. It was not until the late nineteenth century and the industrialization of food, along with the widespread development of the railroads, that rural people, in particular, could cease depending upon their own preserving skills.

Smoking consists of hanging fish or meat over a smoldering, smoking fire so that the flavor is enhanced by the smoke and sealed in. Much of the actual preserving is accomplished by the preliminary act of soaking the fish in either

dry salt or brine (salt water). There are two forms of smoking: "cold" smoking and "hot" smoking. With cold smoking the intention is simply to flavor and seal the fish; with hot smoking the fire is hotter (although still smoky), and the food is cooked as well as smoked.

The wood used to produce the smoke is often in sawdust form, especially for cold smoking. The choice of wood is important – oak is favored because of its sweetness. Hickory is another favorite. African hardwoods are unsuitable – as is any wood that smells acrid or "antiseptic" when burned.

A common structure for a small commercial smokehouse will include a pair of brick ovens, with a space at the bottom for the smoldering sawdust, and detachable metal bars from which to hang the fish. The smoke escapes from

<u>CLEANING AND CURING FISH</u>
Salmon are filleted and prepared for dry curing in salt before smoking.

<u>PREPARED HERRINGS</u>
Herrings are split from head to tail and hooked or threaded onto movable rails.

<u>A HOME SMOKER</u>
Simple but effective, home smokers can take several fish at one time.

the top of the smokehouse via a chimney or a series of ventilation holes. Nearby there will be a water supply and facilities for cleaning and salting the fish.

Smoking can be done at home following the same basic principles. There are a variety of commercially available home smokers consisting, usually, of a lidded box with ventilation holes, a grill, for laying out the fish, and a container at the bottom for sawdust. The aim is to hold the food in a steady stream of smoke. The methods described here, using a home smoker, can be applied to any number of fish, but fresh herring, trout, and mackerel are a popular choice. They can be smoked in batches of two or three in an average-sized home smoker. A fillet of salmon could also be comfortably accommodated, or, alternatively, a dozen oysters. Herring

makes a particularly tasty first attempt.

The first stage in smoking herring is to split and gut it. The aim is to split the fish almost in two, so that it opens up like a book. Lay the herring on a stable work surface; using a sharp filleting knife, spear into the fish halfway between the head and tail, and cut along the backbone. Pull the knife toward and through the head, using the backbone as a guide. Then pull the knife back toward the tail. Try to avoid cutting the herring completely in two. Be careful when pulling the knife toward you. Open out the fish leaving the backbone intact.

Snip out the gills with scissors, then slide the knife under the guts and remove them. Clean the fish in a sink or bowl, under cold running water.

Now cure the herring in salt. Dry curing – putting fish into dry salt rather

126

ROWS OF BLOATERS
*Herrings, soaked in brine and smoked whole,
are known as bloaters.*

FILLETS OF SALMON
*Perhaps the best-known of all smoked
products, salmon turns rich gold in color.*

than brine – dries the fish fast and re-quires a relatively short smoking time. The process of salting and smoking re-duces the weight of the fish overall by between 12 and 20 percent. Therefore, weighing the herring at each stage pro-vides an approximate guide to the length of time it should remain salting and, later, smoking. However, much depends upon personal taste. Also, the weather affects the smoking – if the air is humid the smoking time is longer.

For dry salting, spread salt in a dish to a depth of 1 in (2.5 cm), lay the fish in it and cover it with another ⅜ in (1 cm) of salt, but less at the tail. Cover the dish with a wooden board (make it sterile by first pouring boiling water over it) and leave in a cool place. Leave it until the fish has dried out a good deal. This might be one or several hours, depend-ing on the size of the fish.

Alternatively, the salting can be done in brine. The proportions of salt and water are about 1¼ lb (570 g) of salt to 5 pints (2.25 liters) of water. Boil the water, then allow it to cool. Take one-third of the water, bring it to the boil again, add the salt, remove it from the heat and stir until the salt is dissolved. Add this to the other two-thirds of the water. Put the herring into the brine. It need not stay longer than four to six hours in the brine, although much depends upon the size of the fish – over-salted fish is terrible. Then drain the fish and pat it dry.

Put the smoke box or portable smoker in a well-ventilated outhouse or shed. Lay out the sawdust over the base of the smoker, light it according to the manu-facturer's instructions and place the fish flat over the grill above the sawdust, which should be smoldering and giving off a heat (for "cold" smoking) of around 79°F (26°C). Steady but only moderate smoke is required.

Make sure the smoke circulates freely around each piece of fish. If there is more than one rack in the smoker, the top rack will be ready before the lower. Smoking can take up to 18 hours. The final color should be a delicate gold.

Take a fish and see if it is smoked right through. Weigh it and see if the weight loss is about right, taste it, feel its texture – which should be slightly moist. The best teacher is experimenta-tion, the individual palate and practice.

Subtle variations of flavor can be achieved by adding sweet-smelling herbs to the brine, or scattering them onto the smoking fire.

CHOCOLATE MAKING

<u>SWEET TEMPTATIONS</u>
Squares of nougat and fudge, as well as fresh
cream pecan fondants (above), can be dipped
in chocolate.

COCOA BEANS ARE THE SEEDS OF the cocoa tree, which grows mainly in Africa and Central America. The beans are processed and treated to produce different kinds of chocolate and cocoa products – the best beans being saved to make the finest chocolate.

Professional *chocolatiers* use couverture chocolate, which is made from the finest ingredients and available in huge blocks from specialist suppliers. In order to produce a professional finish the right materials and tools need to be used. There is no substitute for a marble slab, which remains constantly cool, and a pan with a round base is essential, together with specialist dipping forks.

The wonderfully glossy finish of the best hand-made chocolates is achieved by first melting and tempering the chocolate. Nuts, fondants, nougat,

marzipan, and many other sweet centers can then be dipped into it.

To temper chocolate, the following ingredients and equipment are needed: a minimum of 2 lb (900 g) of the best-quality chocolate, to achieve sufficient depth for working; a round-based chocolate pan; a large pan of hot water that the round-based pan can rest over but not in; a marble slab approximately 3 x 2 ft (90 x 60 cm); a dog-leg palette knife and metal paint scraper; a candy thermometer, marked up to 160°F (71°C); and a set of dipping forks.

First, break the chocolate into small pieces and put it in the round-based pan over the water. Stir the chocolate constantly with a wooden spoon over a gentle heat until it has all melted to a smooth consistency. The temperature of the chocolate must never exceed 120°F

(49°C). Remove the pan from the heat and stir to ensure that the chocolate is all at the same temperature.

Pour half the chocolate onto the marble slab. Temper the chocolate by working it on the slab, turning it with the palette knife and paint scraper, until the mixture starts to thicken. Return the chocolate to the pan and stir it thoroughly. Take the temperature of the chocolate in the pan with the thermometer. It is crucial that the chocolate be at a certain temperature before you start to work with it. The working temperature for bitter chocolate is 89°F (31.5°C), for milk chocolate, 87°F (30.5°C). If the mixture is too hot, repeat the tempering process; if it is too cold, replace the pan over the hot water and start again.

Once the chocolate has been tempered correctly it is ready to be used for dip-

PRALINE SWIRLS
The finest quality chocolate is bought in huge slabs to make these creamy pralines (left).

OVAL ORANGE CREAMS
Basic fondant has been flavored with orange, and shaped ready for dipping.

TEMPERING CHOCOLATE
The tempering process (left), always carried out on a marble slab, requires practise.

ping the centers. To do this, place the pan of tempered chocolate on a metal trivet or folded cloth, away from the marble slab. Take a dipping fork, and pick up and then drop a prepared center into the pan. Turn the center over with the fork to make sure that it is completely covered with chocolate, and then lift it out gently, tapping the fork handle on the side of the pan to remove the surplus chocolate. Draw the base of the chocolate across the edge of the pan, and lower it onto a baking sheet covered with waxed paper. Repeat this process until all the centers are covered. Leave the chocolates to set in a cool, dry place.

Fondant centers are always extremely popular, and fresh cream pecans are particularly good. Stored in a cool place (not a refrigerator) they will last for a maximum of two to three weeks.

FRESH CREAM PECAN FONDANTS
*Strips of pecan creams are cut into bite-size
pieces and then dipped.*

COMMERCIAL COVERING
*Enrobing is a mechanical process, dipping is
the traditional hand-made finish.*

For a basic fondant cream you will need 3½ cups (790 g) granulated sugar, 5 fl oz (150 ml) liquid glucose, and 10 fl oz (300 ml) water. Fondant mixture can be stored, almost indefinitely, in a plastic bag in a cool place (not a refrigerator). To make the fresh cream pecans you will need 6 tablespoons (85 g) unsalted butter, 3 oz (85 g) basic fondant cream, 2 oz (55 g) heavy cream, 8 oz (225 g) white chocolate, and a quantity of shelled pecan nuts.

Prepare the basic fondant first. Place the granulated sugar, liquid glucose, and water in a large, thick-bottomed saucepan, cover with a lid, and heat gently until the sugar has dissolved completely. To make sure that no undissolved grains of sugar remain, wipe down the sides of the pan with a wet pastry brush. Once the sugar has dis-

solved, boil the mixture quickly to 240°F (115°C), testing the temperature with a jam thermometer. Then remove the pan from the heat, and pour the fondant onto a marble slab, leaving it to cool to about 100°F (38°C).

With a metal paint scraper, turn the fondant over on the slab, keeping it close to the center, until it all becomes opaque. Continue turning until it begins to show signs of setting. Place the fondant in a bowl, cover it with a damp cloth pressed well down, and set it aside for at least 24 hours before use.

Fondant can be thinned down with syrup if it gets a bit too thick, but never use water. Thinning syrup is easy to make. Dissolve 1 lb (450 g) granulated sugar in 10 fl oz (300 ml) of water in a thick-bottomed pan over gentle heat. Cool and bottle for use as necessary.

The fresh cream pecan filling can then be made in the following way. Place the butter in a food processor and beat it until it is softened. Place the white chocolate in a bowl over hot water to melt. Slowly add the fondant to the butter in small pieces, beating all the time. Then add the cream, a teaspoon at a time. Mix it all together well. Finally, and very slowly, add the white chocolate, which has been thoroughly melted but is only slightly warm, taking care not to curdle the mix. As soon as the mixture is thoroughly blended, switch off the processor. Fill a piping bag (fitted with a ½ in [1.2 cm] plain nozzle) with the fondant mixture and pipe it onto waxed paper in long strips. Cut the strips into bite-size pieces, and top each with a whole pecan nut. Dip in the tempered chocolate as described earlier.

PRESERVES

THE FINEST INGREDIENTS
*Home-made jellies and curds are not only
satisfying to make but mean that fruits can be
enjoyed months after picking.*

JELLIES, JAMS, MARMALADES AND fruit spreads are all methods of preserving fruit with sugar. In one form or another, fruit preserves have been known and recorded since antiquity; the Roman writer Columella, writing about quinces, referred to a quince jam, and also to a pear conserve made with boiled-down wine and water. The grape was an important source of sugar to ancient peoples, and grape juice was frequently used as a sweetening substance. However, only when sugar was cheap and freely available did preserves become widely consumed. Both cane and beet sugar were introduced relatively recently: the Venetians were among the earliest refiners of cane sugar in Europe, in the fifteenth century – beet sugar was not discovered until 1747. In Russia, tea-drinkers would customarily eat spoonfuls of jam as a sweetener with strong black tea.

In pre-industrial times when the majority of people lived off the land, preserving summer produce for winter use was a necessity rather than a luxury. An array of home-made preserves on the larder shelves became a sign of good housekeeping, proof that full use was being made of the gluts of fruit as they came into season. Today, although innumerable commercial brands are available, many people still prefer to make their own. Aside from being economical, home-made preserves have the great advantage of being made only from fruit and sugar, unlike most store-bought varieties, which generally include other coloring, sweetening, and preservative agents.

In addition to well-tried favorites such as strawberry and raspberry jam or apple jelly, it is worth making more unusual preserves, using fruit grown in the garden or gathered in the country. Some of the possibilities include mulberry, loganberry, and pear and pineapple jam; or cranberry, gooseberry, quince, crab apple, sloe, or spiced country jelly (made with elderberries, blackberries, damson plums, apples, and a mixture of spices); or even herb jellies with the tang of mint, sage, tarragon, or rosemary.

In a small-scale commercial operation, preserves can be produced successfully in batches of 20–24 lb (9–11 kg), but for everyday preserve-making batches of about 6 lb (2.7 kg) are the easiest to handle. The secret of making preserves lies first in the quality of the fruit: it should be slightly under-ripe –

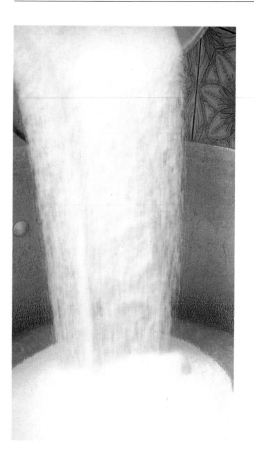

MAKING GRAPEFRUIT MARMALADE
*Sugar is added to the grapefruit mixture,
stirred and then left to dissolve.*

picked early in the season, not at the end. When the fruit is slightly under-ripe and in good condition it contains in its cell walls a natural setting agent called pectin, which is released with the natural acid of the fruit when it is boiled with sugar. The sugar concentrates as the mixture boils and combines with the fruit's pectin into a mass which eventually reaches "setting point." The setting point for jams, jellies, and marmalades is generally 220°F (105°C), measured with a sugar thermometer, but the setting point can also be tested by dropping a teaspoon of the mixture onto a cool saucer. The mixture is left to cool for several minutes, during which time it forms a skin. The skin should wrinkle slightly when your fingertip is pushed across the surface.

The fruit used for preserving should be dry. The water content in damp fruit dilutes the pectin and acid, so that the fruit must be boiled longer, thus losing its color and flavor. The proportion of sugar to fruit varies according to the type of fruit used. The strongest-flavored preserves are made from the sharpest fruit, which dominates the sweetness of the sugar.

There is no need for a special battery of equipment for making jams, jellies, and marmalades. The first essential is a good heavy-gauge preserving pan – not too large as it will be difficult to handle. A sharp knife or shredder is required for marmalades. A sugar thermometer may be used, clipped to the side of the preserving pan. A jelly bag, scalded before use, is needed for making jellies. Other necessary equipment includes: jars (previously sterilized by being placed, partially filled with water, in a shallow pan of water and simmered for 15 minutes), and paraffin for sealing.

GRAPEFRUIT MARMALADE
4 medium-sized grapefruit
2 lemons
5½ pints (2.5 liters) water
12 cups (2.7 kg) sugar

These quantities make approximately 8½ lb (4 kg) of marmalade.

Cut the grapefruit and lemons into quarters. Using a sharp knife, scoop out all the flesh, together with any pith.

Shred the peel as finely as possible, and cook with 1¾ pints (800 ml) of the water for 30 minutes or until tender.

In a separate saucepan, put all the pith, seeds, flesh, and juice with 3¾ pints (1.7 liters) of the water and simmer gently for 1½ hours. Strain the

<u>READY FOR POTTING</u>
Once the marmalade has reached setting point
it can be poured into jars.

<u>SEALING THE JARS</u>
A disk of waxed paper can be used for sealing
instead of paraffin.

liquid from the flesh and seeds into the shredded peel, using a sieve and pushing some of the pulp through it.

Transfer this mixture into a larger open saucepan or preserving pan. Add all the sugar and stir until completely dissolved. Raise the heat and bring the marmalade to a fast rolling boil, stirring occasionally.

Test for setting point, then remove the mixture from the heat and stir in any froth. When it has cooled down enough for the fruit to stay in suspension, pour it into dry, sterilized jars.

Seal each jar with paraffin, in the usual way (for instructions, consult a good, general cookbook).

HERB-APPLE JELLY
4 lb (1.8 kg) apples
3³/₄ pints (1.7 liters) water
granulated sugar*
strained lemon juice*
fresh herbs, such as sage, tarragon,
or rosemary*
*For quantities see below.

Roughly chop the apples and put them into a preserving pan. Cover with the water and simmer gently until soft. Strain the cooked apples through a scalded jelly bag. Measure the juice.

For each pint of apple juice add 1 lb (450 g) of sugar and 3 tablespoons of lemon juice. Return all the ingredients to the preserving pan and bring to the boil. Boil rapidly for about 10 minutes until setting point is reached.

Allow the jelly to cool for a few minutes. Add the herbs (approximately 2 tablespoons, chopped, for each pint of jelly; or one sprig of rosemary per jar). Stir the jelly and pot it immediately.

<u>STRAINING JELLIES</u>
Do not squeeze the jelly bag while the juice is
dripping through — it will cloud and ruin the
appearance of the jelly.

FRESH LEMON CURD
To make lemon curd first melt together butter,
sugar, and lemon juice and rind.

Fruit "curds" are a traditional British delicacy. These are made by a different method from that used for jellies and jams, and they keep for a shorter period, since they contain fresh eggs and butter. The eggs cause the curd to thicken and, as when making egg-thickened sauces, particular care must be taken to prevent them curdling.

Limes, grapefruits, and oranges all make delicious curd but the favorite is lemon curd. A maximum of 5 lb (2.3 kg) can be made in one batch; in larger quantities the mixture will be unevenly heated through, and is likely to curdle. The necessary utensils, apart from jam jars, are a large solid-based saucepan and a wooden spoon. A double boiler is sometimes recommended for making lemon curd but is unnecessary as long as the heat is kept low and the mixture is

<u>A THICK AND CREAMY CONSISTENCY</u>
*In order to make perfectly smooth lemon curd
it must be stirred continuously.*

<u>BOTTLING AND STORING</u>
*Because lemon curd is made with butter and
eggs it must be eaten within one month.*

stirred constantly and tested frequently for thickness on the spoon.

LEMON CURD

3 lemons
3 eggs
8 tablespoons or ¼ lb (125 g)
butter or margarine
1 cup (225 g) granulated sugar

These quantities make approximately 1½ lb (675 g). The lemon curd will keep for about a month if it is stored in the refrigerator.

Grate the rind and squeeze the juice from the lemons. Whisk the eggs in a small bowl. In a heavy-based saucepan melt the butter or margarine, sugar, lemon juice and rind over medium heat, stirring continuously until the sugar is dissolved. When the mixture is fairly hot, but not boiling, add the beaten eggs all at once. Stir continuously with a wooden spoon over low-to-medium heat until the mixture thickens and coats the spoon (two to three minutes). The temptation to desert the saucepan to do something else while the mixture is heating should be strictly resisted. If in doubt, remove the saucepan from the heat as soon as the lemon curd begins to approach the consistency of a thick sauce; the mixture will continue cooking in the pan for two to three minutes.

Remove the pan from the heat when the mixture has thickened, and pour the curd into sterilized jars. Save a little to top up the jars later, as the curd shrinks noticeably as it cools.

When the mixture is cold, cover each jar with a circle of waxed paper and a lid. Label each jar with the date. Store them in the refrigerator.

<u>A TEA-TIME FAVORITE</u>
*A delicious way to eat lemon curd, jams, and
jellies is spread on freshly baked, home-made
bread.*

CIDER MAKING

<u>RIPE AND JUICY APPLES</u>
*Apples for cider making do not need to be in
perfect condition – bruises and over-ripeness
all add to the flavor.*

THERE ARE AT LEAST HALF A DOZEN varieties of apple particularly suited to cider making, all of which are closely related to the wild crab apple and have a bitter-sharp taste. Naming them is difficult, because as old varieties die out, they are replaced by others and often one type of apple is known by different names in each locality. Some are grown on standard trees, which take about five years to mature and provide suitable fruit, and some are grown on bushes, taking two years. The crop is gathered in early autumn, when the apples have reached a point of over-ripeness and drop naturally to the ground. At this time they are at their juiciest and are full of sugar, which is the essential ingredient for the fermentation required for making hard cider.

Apple-gathering is done with a small,

easily maneuvered tractor with wire bins attached; from this field vehicle the fruit is loaded into large trailers and delivered to the cider press. Some cider producers grow all their own fruit, whereas others buy in from neighboring farms; most producers use local fruit. In Britain, cider is made in the West of England, where the soft climate and lush valleys of the sandstone country provide conditions particularly suited to cider-apple growing. The best position for an orchard is on a gentle slope facing the full morning sun, protected from cold winds, and thus less liable to damage caused by frost.

At the cider house, apples are tipped into a walled loading bay which slopes toward a water-filled gully. The apples at the bottom of the pile fall into the gully and are carried along and onto a

conveyor belt, which rises steeply to take them up to the funnel of the mill. During this process the apples are washed to remove dirt. The mill, or crusher, is like a giant food grinder which reduces the fruit to an applesauce-like consistency by means of giant rotary blades. The crushed fruit drops down a wide wooden shute, in amounts regulated by the cider maker, to fill square, slatted, hardwood trays. These trays were traditionally lined with burlap but now an open-mesh polyester fabric is used; this is folded over the pulp to encase and strain it. A stack of twelve trays filled to capacity is called, in England, a "cheese;" this is wheeled into position in the press on short rails which can be linked and repositioned manually, somewhat like a small shunting yard.

When a three-man cider press is

THE LOADING BAY
*Before being pulped the apples pass down a
shute and are thoroughly washed.*

STACKS OF TRAYS
*The pulped apple is poured into trays —
twelve full trays are known as a "cheese."*

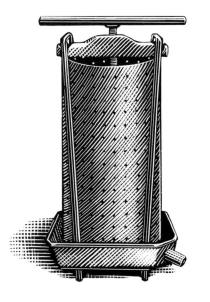

A DOMESTIC APPLE PRESS
*A small winepress can be used for pressing
apple pulp.*

working smoothly it will fill three cheeses an hour and press two thousand gallons (nine thousand liters) in an eight- to ten-hour day. The modern press operates by hydraulic power which is exerted equally over the tray surface. (This kind of press replaced the manual wooden or, later, cast-iron screw.) During pressing the juice is collected in a large tray at the base and is then carried by hose directly to an underground storage tank; when the tank is full the juice is pumped across to a second cider house, where it is transferred to wooden barrels. Mechanized pumps have speeded up this process considerably; previously, wooden scoops, pails, and funnels were used.

Cider is best fermented in huge oak or chestnut barrels called "puncheons" and "pipes." They are first steam-cleaned, then filled to the brim, corked and set on their sides in a cool, well-ventilated place for up to ten months. The cider ferments naturally, without the addition of yeast, and "works" making a constant stream of tiny bubbles whose hiss is clearly audible if the bung, or stopper, is lifted. The flavor and quality of cider depend on the blend of apples used and the fermentation period. One-year-old table cider is fresh and appley, whereas vintage cider can be described as more mellow; both come in grades of dry, medium-dry, and medium-sweet. At the end of the ten-month fermentation period the table cider is pumped out into various casks and containers. Vintage cider is fermented longer, perhaps for two or three years; and the sediment is "racked off" (syphoned off) several times during this

APPLE PULP

The supply of pulp to the trays is carefully regulated before pressing.

PRESSING OUT THE JUICE

The juice is extracted under pressure and is eventually transferred to wooden barrels.

A GLASS OF CIDER

In England, home-made cider is traditionally still and not sparkling.

period for greater purity.

Cottage cider can be made at home, from the following ingredients: 12 lb (5.4 kg) garden apples (a mixture of sweet, sharp, and dry, if possible); 9½ pints (4.5 liters) water, spring water if possible; 3 cups (675 g) granulated sugar; 3 cups (450 g) raisins; and 1 tablet of all-purpose wine yeast (this is optional, it speeds fermentation). These ingredients will make approximately 1½ gallons (5.5 litres) of cider.

Wash and grind the whole apples, or chop them finely; alternatively, put them through a miniature winepress or a food processor. Put the fruit in a very large mixing bowl, ceramic bread bin or plastic fermenting bin (as used by home winemakers). Warm the water and pour it over the apples. Chop the raisins and add them with the sugar; stir the mix-

ture well. If using a yeast tablet, add it last. Cover the mixture with a lid or a board and leave to stand in a warm place for two weeks, stirring and pushing the pulp down daily.

Strain the pulp into a bowl, using an improvised filter made from two layers of cheesecloth or an old, thin, dish towel suspended from the four legs of an upturned stool or beneath a stepladder. Squeeze the pulp lightly and allow the juice to drip through slowly. Syphon it off into fermentation jars, insert an air-lock, and leave the cider to ferment to a standstill in a warm kitchen. Remove the cider to a cool place one month before bottling. Use strong bottles, preferably the type used for sparkling wine, and tie the corks down. Store the cider as long as possible before drinking; the longer it is left, the better it will be.

COTTAGE CIDER

Cider is usually kept in stoneware flagons stopped with a cork.

BASKETRY

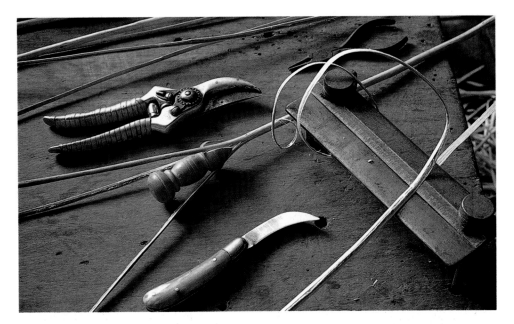

<u>WILLOW COOLING MAT</u>
The basket-maker uses stripped willow and
traditional tools to make a mat (right) for
cooling home-made cakes and bread.

BASKETRY IS AN ENORMOUSLY VER-satile and useful craft. Many things – indeed, most things – have been made with it, from houses and fences to shoes, utensils, and even clothing. No sophisticated equipment is needed, and the materials are lightweight and easy to find. The earliest baskets were probably made from twigs cut with flints. The style of basket-making found in any country usually reflects the local vegetation. In Scandinavia, for example, broad bands of split pine and birch bark are woven together to give the baskets a bold elegance; distinctive African baskets are often made of grass, which is fine enough to create intricate woven patterns and delicate textures.

Although many materials can be used for basket-making, willow has long been one of the most popular, because it

grows well from cuttings and yields an annual harvest. It can also be grown on marshy land unsuitable for other crops.

The willow is cut in winter when the sap is down, and left to stand in water (if it is to be stripped) until early summer, when it starts to shoot and can be stripped of bark. Then it is left to dry in the sun for a day. Unstripped or "brown" willow is also used, but it looks rougher in appearance and is more difficult to clean. It is not soaked, but is left to dry for several months.

The three most common ways of making a basket are coiling, "stake and strand," and framed baskets, which are the oldest. The frames, which form the skeleton of the basket, are often made from undried willow, which is still pliable. The frames are left to dry, then stakes are introduced between the

frames, and the remaining area is filled in with weaving. Coiled baskets are built up from a core material which is joined by vertical stranding, known as lipwork. Stake and strand baskets consist of a base and several uprights, around which the weaving is worked.

The cooling mat shown here is made from "white" or stripped willow. Lengths of willow are usually sold in very large standard bundles; you will need to obtain a 2¼ lb (1 kg) bundle of 3 ft (1 m) willow of the highest quality, and one piece of 6 ft (2 m) willow, measuring about ⅜ in (1 cm) in diameter at the thick or "butt" end. The tools required are: a basket-maker's cleave for splitting the willow, a shave (which is like a plane), a bodkin or awl, garden shears, round-nosed pliers, a pruning knife or sharp penknife, water, a dom-

HARVESTING WILLOW
Willow is gathered in winter when the sap is low. It is usually dried before use.

SOAKING THE BUNDLES
Lengths of willow are dipped in water before use to make them pliable.

estic plant sprayer, and some sacking.

Begin by selecting six willows (plus a few spares) from the bundle; the most even and blemish-free are best. Soak these in water for an hour and leave them to "mellow" under damp sacking for several hours longer.

Half an hour before beginning work, place the single long willow in water to soak. When it has finished soaking, gently flex it to make it pliable. Cut a length from the butt end to make a hoop about 10 in (25 cm) in diameter with some overlap. Trim the butt end so that the last 3 in (7.5 cm) taper. Trim the opposite side of the other end in the same

THE WORKROOM
Bundles of stripped willow are stacked against a wall (right).

THE WORKROOM
Bundles of stripped willow are stacked against a wall (right).

CHOOSING THE LENGTHS
For baskets and trays only willow in top condition is selected.

way, so that when a hoop is formed the two tails fit together perfectly.

The tails are joined with a "skein," which is made from a thin willow from the bundle, split in three with the cleave. Pull one of the split lengths through the shave several times until it is paper-thin. Make the finished skein from the outside of the willow and it is certain to bend in the right direction.

Dip the skein in water then bind it around the joint, starting at the center, then working to the right and then back to the middle, making a broad cross over the earlier binding. Work it out to the left and finish back at the center. The binding should be firm but not too closely spaced. This is the first demonstration of the basket-maker's engineering skill in making each construction as light, and as strong, as possible. To

ATTACHING WILLOWS TO THE HOOP
*An odd number of willows is bound carefully
to the rim of the mat.*

SEPARATING THE UPRIGHTS
*Two rows of fitching are worked to secure the
uprights in position.*

secure the binding, use the bodkin to push the end of the skein back through the joining, then trim the end close to the work. Gently ease the hoop around the rim to make sure that it is regular.

Next, select an odd number of willows from the bundle; 17 were used on the cooling mat shown here. They should be as evenly matched as possible and should measure about ⅛ in (3 mm) at the butt end. If there is a slight variation, use the thickest in the middle of the cooling mat and grade the rest outward on both sides.

Cut a tail, called a "scallom," 4 in (10 cm) in length in the butt end of each

OVERSEWING TO FINISH
*A pair of willows bind the uprights to the top
edge of the hoop.*

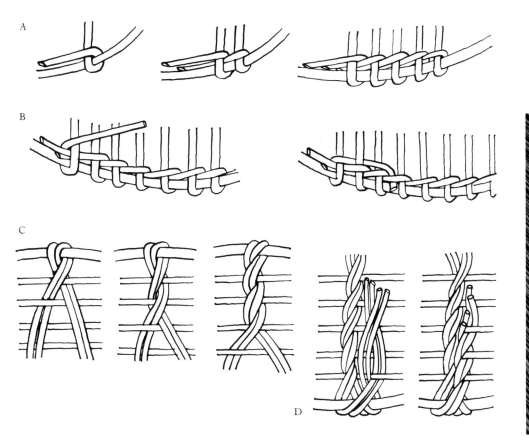

A

B

C

D

BINDING AND FITCHING TECHNIQUES
Binding to the hoop (a) and finishing-off (b);
fitching (c) and finishing-off (d).

BASKET-MAKER'S ART
The cooling mat exemplifies many of the skills
practised by the basket-maker.

piece of willow on the curved or "belly" side. This is done by making a cut in the butt end and then pulling the tail away.

Dip the willows in water before working them. Hold the hoop with the thickest part on the right-hand side and the joining at the bottom and then bind the willows onto the hoop working from right to left, covering the joining as you do so. Lay each willow across the hoop with the heel of the scallom on the rim, then twist the tail around the hoop and back up and over itself, finally tucking it against the inside edge of the rim. As more willows are added, align the tails flat next to each other to fill the bottom part of the hoop and disguise the join. Cut off any tails that stick out beyond the rim, except the last, which should be threaded back over and under several uprights and then cut off.

Pull the thin ends of the uprights together at the top, and cut them off so that they overlap the rim by 1–2 in (3–5 cm).

The next stage is "fitching;" this separates the uprights and fills in the center of the tray. Take two of the willows that have been mellowing under the sacking, hold them together at a point about a third of the way along, and roll them between your fingers to check that the diameters match. Turn the two pieces of willow top to tail. Hold the hoop with the thinnest side to your left, and then bend the pair of willows over the rim of the hoop to the left of center.

Thread the willows between the uprights, under and over each other, keeping the willows taut throughout. At the end of the row, bring the lower willow up around the hoop. Turn the upper willow around the end upright, which

should be held on top with the thumb to prevent it from snapping. Nicking the fitching willow with a fingernail helps it to bend. Weave the ends back through the uprights above the fitching for a little way, then squeeze them close to the fitching with pliers and cut them off. A plant spray can be used to keep the fitching willow pliable. Make a second row of fitching to the right of center.

When both rows of fitching are complete, tie the ends of the uprights onto the rim with a pair of previously soaked willows. With one willow bind them from the center to the right with an oversewing stroke, catching the tail of the binding willow in the strokes under the rim. Trim the uprights to follow the curve of the mat. Repeat with the second willow on the left-hand side so that a cross stitch is formed at the center.

DRIED FLOWERS

<u>LASTING BEAUTY</u>
*The delicate hues of dried flowers and grasses
can be used in a multitude of combinations
and always harmonize.*

FLOWERS ARE USUALLY THOUGHT of as ephemeral, and yet, when ancient Egyptian tombs were opened by archeologists, floral wreaths were found among the items provided for the journey to the next world. The flowers, though faded to a papery brown, had survived for over a thousand years.

Eastern cultures valued flowers for their beauty long before the West saw them as having more than merely medicinal and culinary virtues. Cultivated gardens started to appear in Western Europe only around the fourteenth century, and interest in plants increased with the discovery of different species and varieties in the New World. Herbalists compiled the information, depicted the plants, and gave instructions on how they should be employed. Nosegays composed of sweet-smelling

dried flowers were thought to protect the possessor from inhaling infection, and from the eighteenth century, the petals of dried flowers, mixed with aromatics, formed the basis of pot-pourri.

The Victorians carried the pressing and drying of flowers much further to become almost an art form. Dried flowers and grasses were used as backgrounds to realistic tableaus of stuffed birds and small animals. In the twentieth century, when artificial flowers and even artificial plants are produced in vast quantities, there has been a revival of interest in the drying and arranging of real flowers, with their inimitable and timeless qualities.

Flowers can be air-dried or dried in a desiccant such as sand, borax, or silica gel. The traditional method of air-drying requires no specialist equipment and

is widely applicable. In his herbal of 1653, the English physician Nicholas Culpeper laid down rules for the picking and drying of flowers which, with a few modifications, are still valid.

As a general principle, flowers with woody stems dry more successfully than those with fleshy stems, but experiment with what is available. Old-fashioned roses dry well and retain their scent, but modern hybrid tea-roses do not. Roses should be picked on a bright day before they are full blown, and their stems should not be too long, because they tend to become brittle. Miniature roses provide an attractive contrast. Peonies dry well, as do delphiniums, larkspur, achillea, dahlias, and zinnias.

The flowers known as immortelles or "everlasting daisies," all have a papery quality when dried. In England the ubi-

OLD ROSES
A roughly woven, shallow basket is a perfect foil for a profusion of roses (above).

quitous *Helichrysum*, or strawflower, is used in almost every dried-flower arrangement produced commercially. Less familiar are *Acroclinium*, a daisy-like flower which comes in pink, white, and dark pink with a black center, which is very striking; *Rhodanthe*, another daisy-like flower; *Xeranthemum*; *Ammobium*, or sandflower; and *Nigella*, which is known as love-in-a-mist when in flower and devil-in-a-bush when the flower has become a seed-pod. Certain perennials, such as sea lavender – a variety of statice – *Anaphalis*, and pearl achillea, are very useful for filling in the background of an arrangement.

COLORFUL DESIGNS
After drying, flowers can be arranged in many ways – including decorative trees.

<u>HANGING FLOWERS</u>
Rhodanthe *and* acroclinium *have been tied
into bunches and hung up to dry.*

All traditional hay meadow grasses, such as foxtail, cat-tail, sweet vernal, meadow fescue, and quaking or totter grass dry well, as do ears of corn, barley, wheat, and oats.

Flowers should be picked just before their prime, because otherwise they tend to disintegrate as they dry. Pick them on a dry day, after the dew has evaporated, but not in the full heat of the midday sun. If flowers are picked after rain, they tend to bleach to an unattractive white. The full length of the stem should be picked; it can always be trimmed later. Hydrangeas should be picked at a later stage than most flowers.

<u>A DRYING SHED</u>
*It is a good idea to set aside a cool, dry area
for arranging and drying.*

WIRED POSIES
Small groups of flowers can be bunched and bound with a single wire (above).

Pick them when the petals are beginning to turn green; otherwise they will curl up in the drying process.

A cool, dry, dark place with some ventilation is ideal for drying. There should be space for the flowers to hang upside down without crowding each other, and they should be placed where they will not be brushed against. They can be hung from narrow-gauge doweling supports or from a stout wire or cord, high up near the ceiling to keep them out of harm's way.

Strip off any leaves from the stems before the flowers are dried, unless – as in the case of *Alchemilla* – the dried

BASIC SHAPING
Posies of flowers, including lavender and gypsophila are fixed into the foam.

BUILDING UP THE ARRANGEMENT
Consider the shape, proportions, and texture
of the elements carefully.

THE FINAL TOUCHES
Peonies are added last to this arrangement; it
is important to get the scale right.

leaves are an attractive feature. Small flowers, such as *Acroclinium*, can be dried in bunches of ten to fifteen stems. Bind the bunches tightly about 1½ in (4 cm) from the base of the stems with a rubber band (this allows for the shrinkage that occurs in drying). Hook an S-shaped wire under the rubber band and over the doweling or wire.

Flowers can be fast-dried in a warm place, such as an oven set at a low temperature, but they must not be stored in a warm place or they will become too brittle. This method is useful because it will preserve intense colors – for example, those of cornflowers. Larger flowers, such as peonies or delphiniums, should be dried individually.

Some flowers, such as hydrangeas and gypsophila, are best dried upright. Crush the base of the stems and set them in about ½ in (1.2 cm) of water, so that the flowers dry gradually.

It is especially important that lavender stems be picked on a hot, dry day because the individual florets are cup-shaped and so retain moisture. Lay sprays of lavender flat on newspaper in a single layer, and bunch them only when they have completely dried.

The time a flower takes to dry depends very much on its size and nature but it usually takes a week or two when it is air-dried. As a rough guide, if the *stem* is dry and rigid, this is a sign that the *flower* has dried thoroughly.

Dried flowers can be used in an infinite variety of ways. The basket shown, takes its inspiration from Elizabethan sources, but the field is wide open to innovation and experiment.

In a simple arrangement – such as one composed of dried grasses – a high-sided glass vase would be perfectly suitable, but a more elaborate arrangement, such as this one, requires an opaque container so that the foundation of florist's dry foam cannot be seen.

Use florist's wire for bunching and elongating the stems where necessary. Arrange the smaller flowers in posies first, either in groups of all one variety or in a mixture of several, depending on the effect sought. (For posies, the stems are held together by a single wire, the ends of which serve to strengthen the stems.) Insert the posies in the dry foam, then push in sprays of filler flowers, and finally add any individual flowers or foliage. Provided it is not exposed to strong sunlight, the dried-flower arrangement will retain its color for about two to three years.

CANDLE MAKING

A STORE OF WAX
*Wax can be bought in granular form, which
is easy to melt down.*

CANDLES ARE THE MOST ANCIENT and appealing of all man-made lights and have long been associated with special occasions and religious festivals. A candle, in essence, is solidified fuel surrounding a wick. The fuel is melted by the heat of the flame, and continuously feeds the flame through the burning wick. Oils from fish or olives, or wax from berries and trees were the fuels used in earliest times. From cave paintings it is known that prehistoric man used a form of candle, and pictures on Egyptian tombs also show primitive candles being used. By the Middle Ages, when candle making had become firmly established as a trade, tallow was the most common raw material. Unfortunately, this animal fat gave off a great deal of smoke and smelled acrid when burned; the alternative fuel, bees-

wax (still one of the finest fuels for candle making), was never plentiful enough to meet the demand.

The nineteenth century saw the mechanization of the candle making industry. As a result, the search for new types of fuel to improve and increase production began. Parraffin wax, a by-product of petroleum oil, proved to be the most significant discovery. It is this fuel, often mixed with stearin (a fatty acid derived from palm oil that makes paraffin wax stronger, stiffer, and slower burning), that is most commonly used by candle makers today.

The wick is as important as the fuel in the making of a candle. The guttering and smoking produced by early candles was overcome in the early nineteenth century by the introducton of braided cotton or bleached and woven linen

wicks, treated with chemicals such as nitrate of bismuth and boric acid.

The two best-known methods of candle making are dipping and molding. Dipping is the older and simpler method. Molding, probably a fifteenth-century development, is popular because virtually any shape of candle can be made, using any household container that will not melt when molten wax is poured into it. Glass, metal, and cardboard are all suitable materials, but plastic is the best for beginners. Experienced candle makers can achieve spectacular results. They use a wide range of decorative techniques involving colored waxes, painting, swirling, layering, surface texturing, such as carving and hammering, and hand-molding techniques, such as braiding, pinching, rolling, and twisting. The

MELTING AND DIPPING
*When the wax has reached the correct
temperature, a length of wick can be dipped.*

DIPPED CANDLES
*A number of candles can be made in any one
session, but they must be left to harden slightly
between dippings. It may take 40 dippings to
complete a candle.*

ROLLED SHEETS OF BEESWAX
Lay a length of wick on the wax, turn in the edge firmly, and roll up.

GLASS MOLDS
The wick is secured in the center of the mold and wax is poured in.

largest free-standing candle in the world, made in Britain in 1989, was 30 ft (9 m) high and 3 ft 6 in (1 m) wide. However, even a beginner at candle making can produce beautiful and unusual candles with a little practise.

Dipped candles are made using simple equipment, and professional results can be achieved. To make three pairs of 9 in (22 cm) candles approximately ½ in (1.2 cm) in diameter, the following materials are required: 6½ lb (3 kg) paraffin wax and three 22 in (56 cm) lengths of ⅓ in (8 mm) wick. The following equipment is also needed: a stove, scales, a dipping can (any heatproof, waterproof container a little taller than the length of the candles to be made), a pan to hold the container, a candy thermometer, a drying rack and a sharp knife for trimming the candles.

The working area should be clear, clean and as draft-free as possible, with all the equipment and materials ready. Begin by putting the wax in the dipping can. Stand the can in a pan of simmering water and place the thermometer in the wax. Heat the wax until it has melted and reached a temperature of 160°F (71°C). It is important to maintain this temperature throughout the dipping process until the required thickness of candle has been reached; otherwise the candle is likely to crack. The wax is like cooking oil and will catch fire if it gets too hot. If the wax does start to overheat and begin to smoke, switch off the heat and leave it to cool. If the wax catches fire, *do not* use water, but smother it quickly with the pan lid. Then remove the smoldering pan from the heat and leave it to cool for ten minutes.

When the wax is ready, fold one of the wicks in half, ready to make two candles. Holding the center of the wick, hang the ends in the wax to a depth of 9 in (22 cm) for one minute to get rid of air and any moisture. Lift out the wick, and straighten the two ends as they cool, squeezing each one between finger and thumb to get rid of any kinks. Hang the wick over a rod or hook for at least one minute to harden. Meanwhile, repeat the process with the other two lengths of wick. This is the wick-priming process and is important to ensure that the finished candle will burn successfully, and to prevent its surface from becoming lumpy. Then maintain a cycle of repeatedly dipping each wick in the wax for three-second periods and then hanging it up for at least one minute before re-dipping. The water in the pan must

PURITY AND LIGHT
Simple, white candles (right) cast a serene light as well as being decorative.

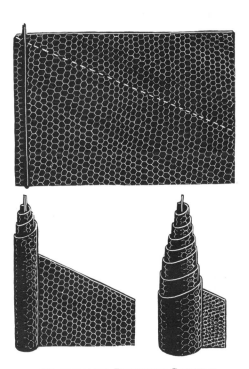

GRADUATED BEESWAX CANDLE
Cut a sheet of beeswax at an angle and begin rolling from the longest side.

not be allowed to run dry so check the level regularly and top up with boiling water, if necessary. Make sure that no water falls into the molten wax and, in particular, that no water drips onto the wick. Continue the dipping cycle until the candles are the thickness you want (this will probably take 40 dippings).

Finally, heat the wax to 180°F (82°C). Dip the pairs of candles into the wax for three seconds each. Cool them for one minute and then repeat. This will give the candles a smooth and glossy finish. Trim the bases with a sharp knife. Hang the candles up for about one hour to set thoroughly.

Always leave newly-made candles for twenty-four hours before using them, and test them in a draft-free place. Trim the wicks to a length of ½ in (1.2 cm) before lighting the candles.

DECORATIVE CRAFTS

STICK DRESSING □ GILDING

CARVED BIRDS □ TOY MAKING □ LEATHERWORK

SPONGEWARE □ STENCILED TILES

STAINED GLASS □ JEWELRY

STICK DRESSING

INTRICATE HAND CARVING
*Hours of work and years of experience go in
to making the most elaborate and decorative
dressed sticks.*

FROM EARLIEST TIMES, WHEN AGRI-cultural communities first kept live-stock, shepherds' crooks and sticks have been a part of rural life. In Europe, during the fifteenth century, however, sticks became fashionable accessories, as well as serving a practical function, and a highly decorated stick indicated high status. In the following centuries many new forms of stick developed, including the walking stick, the shooting stick, and the sword stick. It was not until the twentieth century that sticks declined in popularity and the craft returned to its origins – to the rural communities.

Until recently, stick dressing has been kept a jealously guarded secret in the hands of a few skilled craftsmen. It is predominantly in the North of England that it has grown from a humble craft into an exacting art.

Simply dressed sticks can be made en-tirely of wood, but in sheep-rearing areas the addition of a horn hand-piece is a natural and challenging elaboration. Any horn from sheep will do, although cow, buffalo, goat, and deer horn have also been carved by experienced stick-dressers. The most sought-after horn, which is also the most difficult to obtain, is that of an old ram. With modern farming techniques, rams are rarely left to live to a ripe old age and die naturally on the hills.

The art of stick dressing lies in achieving a harmonious balance betwen shank (shaft) and head – years of ex-perience and a good eye yield remark-ably beautiful results. Of the many tra-ditional styles of stick carved, a plain walking stick with a horn head is the most suitable for a beginner. Even so,

this type of stick can take many hours to carve (an experienced stick-dresser could spend 30 to 40 hours on one).

Ideally, a plain head for a walking stick requires about 8–10 in (20–25 cm) of solid horn, preferably from a four- or five-year-old ram. A "fancy" carved stick requires a broader, fuller horn. Freshly gathered horn must be seasoned for at least a year before use.

Hazel is the preferred wood for the shank of the stick, but holly, cherry, apple, pear, ash, or blackthorn can also be used. Shanks should be cut in mid-winter, when the tree is dormant and should be as straight as possible with a slight taper at one end. The length of the shank is a matter of personal taste and comfort, but approximately 4 ft (1.2 m) is a good choice. Season it, too, for at least a year before working.

A =3½ in (9 cm); B = 3 in (7.5 cm);
C = ½ in (1.2 cm); D = 1 in (2.5 cm);
E = 1 in (2.5 cm); F = 1¼ in (3.2 cm).

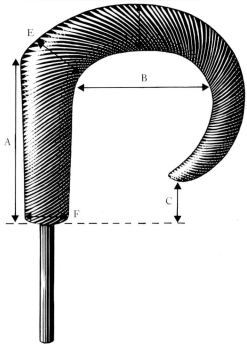

A BUCKETFUL OF HORN

Horn must be seasoned for about a year before
it can be successfully worked (left).

It is possible to straighten a slightly bent shank after seasoning. Warm the shank with a hot-air paint stripper (or over a gentle candle flame) and pull any irregularities straight in a vise. Take care not to burn the bark; use aluminum foil to protect it, if necessary.

Apart from a suitable ram's horn and shank, the equipment required to make the stick is usually to be found in a well-stocked workshop. To shape and compress the horn you will need a strong vise, a hot-air paint stripper (or candle flame), two or three rasp files, a number of finer files of different grades, a hacksaw, a coping saw, a handsaw, a cramp, woodworker's chisels, a sharp pocket knife, and a pencil. Also, small blocks of wood in various shapes and some curved pieces of steel are useful for shaping and supporting the horn. To

<u>A HAND-PIECE</u>
A basic shape is cut, and a clear outline drawn onto the horn.

<u>SHAPING THE HORN</u>
After gentle heating, horn can be manipulated and compressed into shape.

<u>FILING AND FINISHING</u>
The horn is carefully filed, smoothed with an emery cloth, and then polished.

join the shank to the hand-piece you will need a hand brace with a ⁵⁄₁₆ in (7 mm) drill bit and a very fine drill bit, a 4 in (10 cm) steel bolt ⁵⁄₁₆ in (7 mm) in diameter, epoxy resin glue, and strong string. To apply the finish, various grades of emery cloth, steel wool, scouring powder, brass-cleaning cream, and varnish are required.

The center, solid, portion of the horn is used for the hand-piece, and the outer layers need to be cut away with a coping saw, leaving a piece about 8 in (20 cm) long. Then mark the horn into three sections with a pencil – 3 in (7.5 cm) for the neck (where the hand-piece joins the shank), 3 in (7.5 cm) for the grip (where the hand-piece curves), and the remainder for the nose.

Heat the horn gently but thoroughly with a hot-air paint stripper, or candle flame, applying the heat to 1 in (2.5 cm) sections, gripping it in the vise, and manipulating and compressing it into shape using the cramp, the small blocks of wood, and the curved pieces of steel. Start from the neck and work slowly around to the nose. The heat must completely penetrate the horn before it can be shaped. If the horn is heated gently enough, it can be shaped several times before it suffers ill effect.

Once the basic shape has been achieved, use the rasps to file away the horn, but do not remove too much.

Using the hand brace fitted with the ⁵⁄₁₆ in (7 mm) drill bit, drill a 2 in (5 cm) deep hole into the core of the horn. Position the bolt, secure it with the epoxy resin, and leave it to dry. The bolt can be bent to ensure that the horn will sit true on the shank. Use the finer files and emery cloth to refine the overall shape.

Then grip the shank in the vise, and, using the ⁵⁄₁₆ in (7 mm) drill bit, drill a 2 in (5 cm) deep hole into the core of the shank so that it aligns with the bolt in the horn. Use the fine drill bit to make an "escape hole" for the glue at the base of the bolt shaft. Bring the hand-piece and the shank together, and glue the bolt into the hole in the shank. Tie a length of string between the crown and the shank, twist it taut, and leave it to dry.

File the horn to the exact diameter and shape of the shank, protecting the shank with tape, if necessary. Complete the shaping with the fine emery cloth. Polish the horn with steel wool, scouring powder, and brass cleaner – in that order – to bring up the translucent quality of the horn. Finally, give the shank three coats of varnish.

GILDING

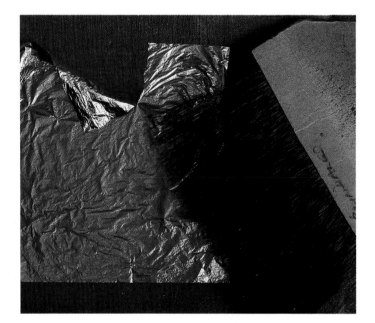

<u>GLORIOUS GOLD LEAF</u>
*The merest breath will disturb a delicate sheet
of gold leaf but once applied to a surface it
will last for many years.*

ONE OF THE MOST APPEALING RAW materials is gold leaf – gold that has been hammered into gossamer-thin sheets for use by gilders, jewelers, and illuminators. The intrinsic value of gold is somehow enhanced by the butterfly-wing fragility of the leaf.

Gilding has a long history. It was especially favored by Byzantine artists as a means of enriching architectural decoration and also as an embellishment to paintings – gold for halos and for the costumes of the more important characters in religious paintings was commonplace. The gold had a devotional significance in such works of art.

During the great flowering of illustrated books and manuscripts in medieval western Europe, gold was applied to the elaborate calligraphic motifs and illustrations. Important pieces of furniture and many types of painting were also gilded. Later, the Baroque style of architecture and decoration brought a lavish use of gold leaf – as did the still-later Neo-classical style, though in a more restrained manner.

One of the most common uses of gilding is on frames. The picture frame has a long pedigree, but not so long as that of the mirror frame, which begins in Egypt about 1300 B.C.

The genesis of the modern picture frame lies in medieval Europe and the free-standing altar paintings of the church. Later, in the seventeenth century, ornately framed paintings helped to satisfy the desire for secular ornament for the homes of the aristocracy and the new middle classes.

For centuries the frame-maker and gilder were anonymous craftsmen working in relatively large workshops. It was usual, from the Middle Ages onward, for various specialists to collaborate. Carvers and molders worked with the "finishers" – men who did the mounting and gilding, and who also gilded furniture and added gold to paintings. It is clear that the gilded frame was valued highly by the client; it was an important part of the painting as a piece of furniture.

There are two forms of gilding – oil gilding and water gilding. Oil gilding is the more durable of the two and is used for decorating furniture, but unlike water gilding, it cannot be burnished (polished). The disadvantage of water gilding is its fragility.

Gilding begins with the preparation of the frame (which is usually wood or plaster). Then comes the "coloring up"

THE BURNISHED FRAME
A gilded mirror (above) is a luxurious addition to a room.

PREPARING THE SURFACE
Layers of gesso are applied to the surface to act as a cushion for the gold leaf. Any brush marks should be smoothed away with fine sandpaper.

<u>APPLYING THE BOLE</u>
Yellow, red, and black Armenian bole are
painted onto the surface of the frame.

<u>READY FOR GILDING</u>
Before the gold leaf is applied, the surface of
the frame must be moistened.

with Armenian bole and the laying of the gold leaf, followed, sometimes, by the process of distressing.

The main material, the gold leaf itself, comes in little books, usually laid on squares of pink paper. A delightful material, which gives a real fillip to the spirit, it is, however, tricky to handle and apt to take flight at the slightest puff of air; avoid breathing heavily on it! For applying gold leaf there are special gilder's tools: a gilder's knife and pad for cutting the leaf and a gilder's tip – a flat, broad brush – for transferring it to the pad and then to the frame.

The gold leaf is applied to a foundation of gesso. This is made by melting animal glue size and a little water together in a bowl. Stand the bowl in a paint can partly filled with water, over heat. The proportions are approxi-

mately one part size to one part water. Sprinkle whiting over the size mixture until it lies just below the surface, then mix them together to form a very thin, creamy paste. The proportions of size, water, and whiting vary, depending on the required degree of hardness; a higher proportion of water produces a softer gesso.

The color that shines through distressed gilding is supplied by Armenian bole, a fine-grained clay paste which is always applied to give the work a very smooth surface. This comes in a variety of colors; for the frame illustrated, yellow, red, and black bole are required. The final burnishing is done with an agate stone set in a handle. The other materials required are denatured alcohol, several fine nylon brushes, medium-grade sandpaper, fine wet-and-

dry sandpaper, and some soft cloths.

The basic technique for gilding frames has not changed much since medieval times. As with all crafts, careful preparation is vital for a professional finish. Begin by passing a medium-grade sandpaper over the frame to roughen the surface slightly and thus provide a "key" to hold the gesso.

Prepare a mixture of hard gesso and apply it with a fine nylon brush. When this coat is dry, another five coats of gesso must be painted on – two medium-hard coats followed by three soft coats. Allow each application to dry before proceeding to the next.

Rub a damp cloth over the frame to smooth away the brush marks and generally clean up the surface. Finally, rub the surface with a piece of fine wet-and-dry sandpaper. The frame is now

LEAVES OF GOLD
Gold leaf (above) is purchased in small books. It is an ambitious investment.

ready for coloring up with the bole.

Brush a layer of yellow bole onto the frame using a soft, fine nylon brush. After the yellow, apply two coats of red. Each layer must be allowed to dry before continuing with the next. At this point there is a choice to be made – namely, which parts of the frame are to be burnished. These parts will be given a coat of black bole. In the example shown, the corners of the frame are burnished, and therefore these areas are coated with black bole. The areas in between are given a coat of thinned, cold size.

When the black bole is dry (but not too dry, leather-hard is about right), burnish it using a brush cut down to a stubble that just extends beyond the shaft of the handle. Use firm (but not undue) pressure and circular motions to give the surface a smooth, shiny patina.

GILDING THE FRAME
*A gilder's tip is used to brush the gold leaf
gently into every contour.*

THE DISTRESSED LOOK
*Part of the gilding can be rubbed away to
give the frame an aged appearance.*

The frame is now ready for gilding. Before laying the leaf upon the frame, lightly rub the area with some cold water mixed with a small amount of denatured alcohol to remove the grease.

To pick up the gold leaf, first gently brush the gilder's tip across a slightly greasy surface, such as your hair or skin. Then scoop up the gold leaf and lay it flat on the gilder's pad. It takes practice to achieve the necessary fluid movement, from scooping up to the pad. Cut the gold leaf to size with the gilder's knife. Pick it up with the gilder's tip and lay it on the moistened surface of the frame. Follow the same procedure around the frame, overlapping the sections as carefully and unobtrusively as possible. Like picking up the leaf, laying it down takes practice; the goal should be a movement that is neither over-cautious nor cavalier. Smooth layering is needed.

Once the frame has been covered, give the corners their final burnish – once, that is, the frame has dried. However, it is important that the frame not be bone dry, because the burnishing of the corners requires the bole beneath the leaf to act as a cushion. About half an hour's drying time is usually plenty. Burnish the corners of the frame, using the agate stone.

When the corners have been burnished, the rest of the frame can then be distressed, if you wish. Work over it with absorbent cotton and denatured alcohol, wearing the gold away to reveal the red bole beneath. Do not overdo the distressing. Think of the process as glazing in reverse; the idea is to maintain the gold "glaze" but let something of the color show through.

SKILLFUL GILDING
*Applying gold leaf to a highly carved surface
requires skill and patience.*

CARVED BIRDS

DECORATIVE WILDFOWL
*Birds, such as the "Preening Pintail
Mallard" (left) can be carved from, and
even mounted on, pieces of driftwood.*

THE DECORATIVE CARVED BIRDS made by today's craftsman have evolved primarily from the tradition of making decoys – lifelike wooden birds used by hunters to lure wildfowl to their hunting grounds.

These carved wooden birds are believed to have originated in the United States among the American Indians, and to have been taken up by the settlers hunting wildfowl in the early nineteenth century. Decoy making was practiced most intensively on the eastern seaboard, where there was a growing market for both meat and feathers among the fashion-conscious, meat-hungry populations of New York, Philadelphia, and Boston. At its peak, the making of decoys was a sizeable industry, with small factories producing thousands of birds a year.

As the seasons changed and different species appeared the hunters would be ready – they had decoys for every type of bird. Sometimes, if a decoy for the required species of bird was not available, the hunter might simply repaint one with a similar body shape.

Although most decoys were produced in factories, some continued to be hand-made by men who earned their living on the coast. These shoremen turned their hand to everything including fishing, boat-building, and beachcombing. They collected driftwood to fashion into birds for the shooting season. Living among birds, they had an intuitive knowledge of how to replicate them and a stock of skills passed on from father to son. These nineteenth-century decoys are now collectors' items.

The unbridled commercial exploita-tion of wildfowl led to the endangering of some species. But new regulations in the early twentieth century curtailed hunting by preventing a duck shot in one state from being sold in another. The decoy industry was ruined, and many thousands of these wooden birds were destroyed. However, some of the more talented hand-carvers survived by making their work more decorative and selling them as ornaments.

Since the 1950s decoys have been pro-duced cheaply from plastic; this marked the end of carving wooden birds for hunting. The contemporary bird carver follows in the decorative rather than the hunting tradition. The pieces are now objects for contemplation, often in-spired by a love of birds and their en-vironment. The motivation is to con-serve rather than destroy nature.

BIRDS IN FLIGHT
*Shafts of light glinting across the spread
wings of these carved birds (left), illuminate
the natural hues of the wood.*

THE CARVER'S WORKSHOP
*Every piece of available space is crowded
with reminders of the seashore.*

The coastal habitat of many of these
birds can be a source of raw materials as
well as an inspiration to the carver – for
example, driftwood picked up along the
shore could be used either as a decorative
stand on which to place the bird or
carved as an integral part of the bird
itself. Any found wood must be given
ample time to dry out before carving
begins. Seasoned scraps of wood from
lumber yards may also be used. Soft-
woods such as pine are ideal as they are
easy to work.

A large repertoire of species, from
tiny shore birds to huge wild swans, can
all be made by the same basic method.
The aim is not to make an exact likeness
of a particular species but to portray a
bird in essence. Carvers tend to work
from memory, drawing on knowledge
gained over years of observing birds in

<u>BIRDS NEW AND OLD</u>
*The concept of carved birds has changed very
little from original decoys (below).*

their natural habitat.

The body and head are always made separately. Profiles of the two pieces are drawn on a block of wood and cut out with a band saw, then worked with files and sandpaper to refine the shape. After the head and body are joined, the markings are painted. Finally, the bird is waxed to give it a luster.

Some pieces may be quite fanciful — drawn in part from the imagination, partly inspired by the smooth curves and postures of a great variety of birds. The "Preening Pintail Mallard" has the shape of a pintail and the markings of a mallard, thus combining the most attractive features of the two birds — but it could be fashioned in any way.

To make the "Preening Pintail Mallard" the following materials and equipment are required: two blocks of lum-

CARVING THE BIRD
A heavy-duty file is used to create the basic body shape.

THE HEAD AND BODY JOINED
The neck forms a smooth, continuous curve and paint disguises the joining.

ber, one at least 20 x 6 x 3 in (50 x 15 x 7.5 cm) for the body and one 2 x 6 x 6 in (5 x 15 x 15 cm) for the head, offcuts of spruce or deal from a lumber yard are ideal for this project; a band saw (if this is not available a fret saw will do); heavy-duty files or coarse sandpaper; finer files or sandpaper; steel wool; a carver's vise (this stands up from the bench enabling the piece to be worked on all sides); a drill with a ³⁄₈ in (1 cm) bit; water-soluble wood glue; a short ³⁄₈ in (1 cm) diameter dowel; a blow torch; 2 dolls' eyes or beads; a small amount of ready-mixed plastic paste; latex paints or watercolor paints and a paintbrush; and wax polish.

To begin, draw the profile of the head and body on the appropriate blocks of wood. The overall length of the carved bird is 20 in (50 cm) and is most pleas-

ACCENTUATING THE WOOD GRAIN
A blow torch is used to add texture to the surface of the wood.

ing in the following proportions – 12 in (30 cm) for the head and body and 8 in (20 cm) for the tail. Ideally, this basic shape is first cut out roughly using a band saw. Alternatively, a professional carpenter would probably be willing to do this initial cutting for a modest fee.

Then work on the head and body separately in the carver's vise to refine the shape. Use heavy-duty files (coarse sandpaper can be used instead) to take off all the rough edges and then to refine the curves of the overall shape. As the shape emerges, change to a finer file or sandpaper, and concentrate on the quality of the finish. Compare the size and curve of the neck on both pieces, to make sure that they fit together well.

Now go over both head and body with a blow torch. It is best to practise on scraps of wood first to avoid setting the

<u>A PERFECT SETTING</u>
*True to nature, these birds are in perfect
harmony with their environment.*

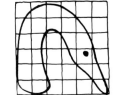

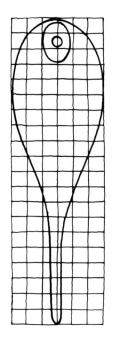

<u>PROFILES OF THE BIRD</u>

work on fire. This part of the process will accentuate the grain of the wood by burning out the soft areas and leaving the harder lines raised. Use sandpaper and steel wool to remove discoloration caused by the blow torch.

Using the drill, make the holes for the eyes in the head, positioning the holes in keeping with the proportions of the bird's head.

Next drill a hole in the base of the head, half the length of the dowel. Squeeze or paint a small amount of glue in a ring around this hole. Place the head on the body with the neck edges matching, then lift it off. The glue will have left a circular mark on the neck; drill into the body in the center of this mark making a corresponding hole half the length of the dowel. Put glue in both the head and body holes, then join the two

pieces with the dowel. Leave to dry.

Fill in any cracks, holes or other irregularities with plastic paste. Put paste in the eye holes and insert the eyes; brush off excess paste.

After the paste has dried, sand the entire surface lightly with fine sandpaper to prepare it for painting; no primer is required. Apply the color, referring to these photographs. Alternatively, paint the bird in colors of your own choice; it is less important to render markings accurately than to create a sense of the bird's plumage.

When the paint is dry, go over the whole piece again with fine sandpaper to remove any bubbles and irregularities. Finally, to tone down the stark effect of the paint, apply a coat of wax, polishing it well with a soft cloth to give the work an attractive sheen.

TOY MAKING

<u>COLORFUL WOODEN MODELS</u>
*Simple shapes and bold colors make these toys
lasting favorites with children
of all ages.*

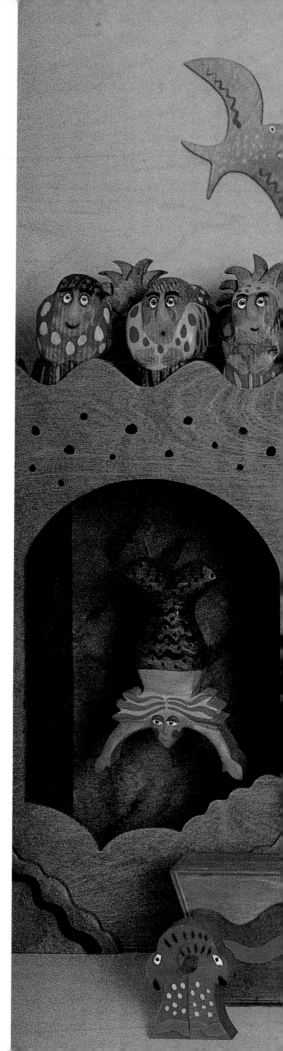

PLAYING IS AN ACTIVITY AS OLD AS humankind, indeed older, for other species play too. But the craft of toy making does not have such a long history – not, that is, the making of toys especially for children. The idea of childhood as a separate state of existence with its own artefacts, clothes, and language is a modern one. As late as the eighteenth century, children were treated as miniature adults, and the toys that survive from that time are either educational, like the elegant bone alphabets of the period, or purely decorative, such as the elaborate but unyielding dolls given to little girls.

But play objects for adults abound, from the earliest stages of all civilizations. Miniature figures in Inuit and African societies were used for ritual, for worship, or simply as a symbolic form of decoration. The miniature furnishings that the Egyptians put into tombs were a way of giving physical substance to their belief in the afterlife. These, however, were objects for playing out an idea, rather than just playing.

The Egyptians did have more functional toys, including marbles, but it is from those symbolic miniature models that the craft tradition of toy making draws a good deal of its inspiration. Unlike many manufactured toys, most hand-made toys do not "do" anything; rather, they come to life – in a way similar to the Egyptians' furniture or the Inuit figure - only when touched by the imagination of the user.

Today there are two main types of craftsman-made toy. The more elaborate kind is part of the model-making tradition that grew up in the

<u>FUN AND GAMES</u>
These lively characters and toy theaters can be played with or kept safe as ornaments.

<u>TRADITIONAL TOYS</u>
Tops, pull toys and Russian dolls are still extremely popular today.

eighteenth century and coincided with an interest in collecting and antiquarianism. The early cabinets of curiosities, forerunners of the modern museum, sometimes included miniature models. The first doll houses were, therefore, often built in the form of such cabinets, and were intended for adults.

The tradition of model-making continues to thrive, though elaborate pieces of craftsmanship are always expensive and often too delicate to withstand much use. By contrast, the folk tradition of toy making is in every sense more robust. Even in the age of plastic, a wooden toy still has the advantage of usually being easy to mend.

It is rare that a wholly new toy is invented. The top, the doll, the hobbyhorse, and the pull toy remain firm favorites, as do toys that involve finding one

thing inside another, such as Russian dolls, Chinese puzzles, and jack-in-the boxes. When a new toy enters the repertoire it can become an international sensation. In France, in 1746, the *pantin*, or jumping jack – a wooden jointed figure that leaped when its string was pulled – became a fad of such astonishing proportions that a law was passed banning the toy.

Although the wooden toys shown here are unlikely to provoke such a craze, they are nevertheless a charming variation on tradition. They combine elements of the bottom-heavy rolling clown, the rocking horse, and the rattle. Bold coloring and a strong outline place them in the mainstream of folk toys.

Unlike elaborate models, this kind of toy can be made relatively quickly and inexpensively. In a modern, commer-

AN ASSORTMENT OF ANIMALS
*These creatures may not be true to life but
they are instantly appealing.*

cial, workshop a craftsman can break the process down into stages and make the toys in batches. The hand-painting ensures that each one will vary slightly.

The toy illustrated on pages 188-89 is a pirate but it can easily be turned into a clown or an ice-cream salesman with cones, or indeed a dozen other characters. Any kind of paint, stain, or varnish can be used (provided it is non-toxic) to give shiny or matte finishes.

The materials and equipment used are simple: a piece of thin cardboard 10 x 5 in (25 x 13 cm); one piece of softwood, preferably pine, 1 in (2.5 cm) thick, measuring 10 x 6 in (25 x 15 cm); one piece of ¼ in (5 mm) plywood, measuring 6 x 2 in (15 x 5 cm); a 3 in (7.5 cm) length of ¼ in (5 mm) dowel; a drill with a ¼ in (5 mm) bit; gouache or acrylic paint for decoration; paint-

PLYWOOD BLANKS
*An egg carton is a very useful means of
storing batches of animal shapes.*

187

Make a cardboard guide for the basic shape (left), drawing in the pirate's features, too. Transfer to the wood block and cut out with a fret saw.

PAINTING THE WOODEN ROCKER
Use non-toxic paint and varnish if the rocker is to be given to a child.

PAIRS OF PARROTS
Paint the parrots with a fine paintbrush. Suggest their wings and beaks – it does not matter if they do not look identical.

brushes; non-toxic matte varnish; sandpaper; wood glue and a fret saw.

First draw the outline of the pirate on cardboard; the features can also be added for reference. Draw around a plate for the outside curve, which should measure 10 in (25 cm) across. Fit the head, arms, and body of the figure into the line of the curve, so that the finished pirate will rock as far as possible. The legs should be thick enough at the middle to weight the figure toward the bottom. Next draw the shape of the parrots onto the cardboard. They should be just under 2 in (5 cm) tall.

Cut out the shapes and use them as templates. Cut the pirate's body from the piece of wood, and four parrots from the plywood. When cutting the body it is essential to maintain an exact right-angle between the side and the edge;

THE PIRATE ROCKER
*No two pirates will be exactly the same; their
individuality is their charm.*

otherwise the toy will not rock. Once the pieces have been cut out, sand down the edges. The upper edges can be rounded, but only take a little off the rocker.

Drill a hole in the back of each parrot's head, ¼ in (5 mm) in diameter and as deep as possible without cutting right through. Drill two more holes, just over ¼ in (5 mm) across, through each of the pirate's hands. Cut the dowel into two pieces, each 1 ½ in (4 cm) long.

Before the final assembly, paint the pirate and the parrots. The effect should be as bright and bold as possible. Leave the pieces to dry, varnish them and then leave them to dry again. Take two of the parrots and glue a piece of dowel into the back of each. When the glue has dried, push the dowels through the holes in the pirate's hands, and glue the other two parrots to the ends.

A CHEERFUL CLOWN
*Many different characters can be made using
the same basic technique. For a clown, make
swinging umbrellas instead of parrots.*

189

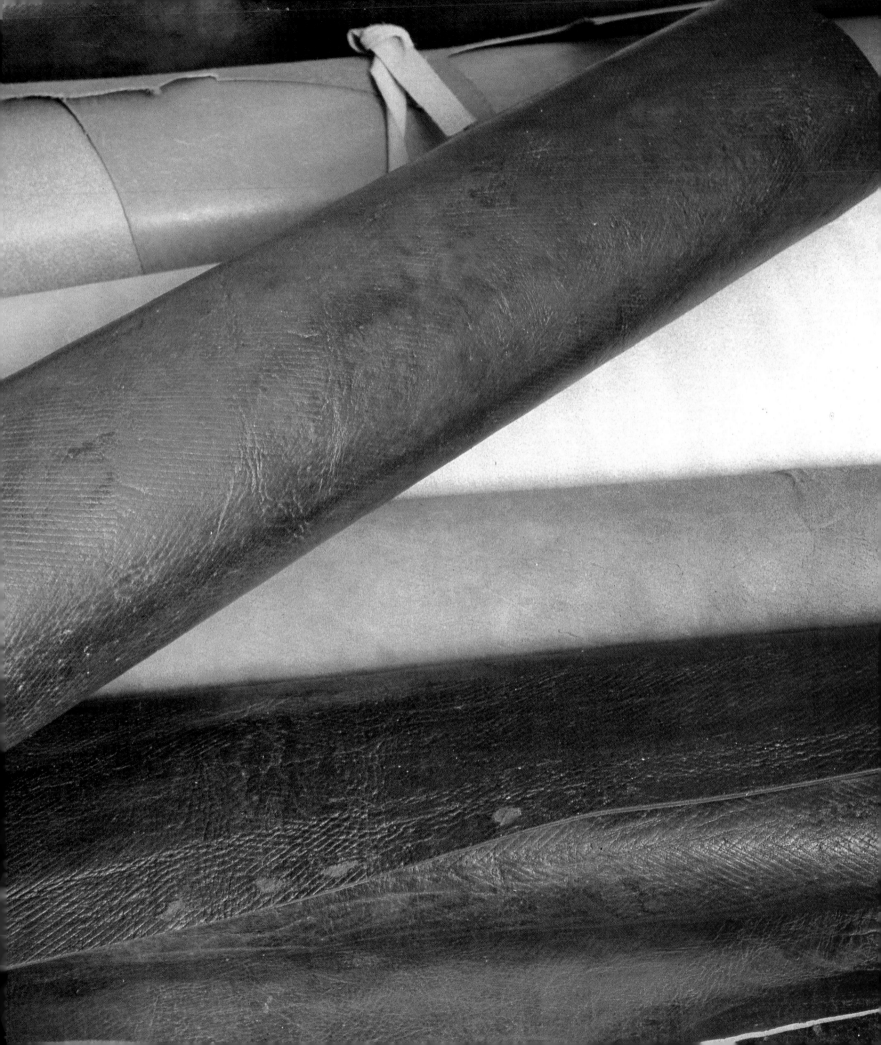

LEATHERWORK

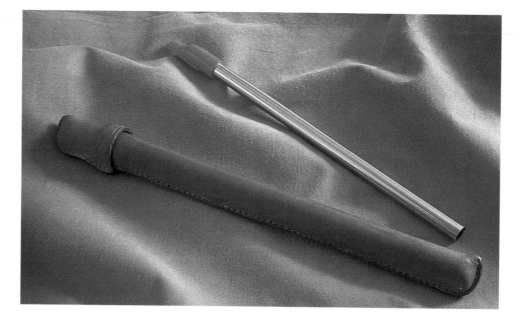

THE WHISTLE CASE
*Vegetable-tanned leather has been used to
make this hand-stitched whistle case. It has
been dyed and polished to a rich sheen.*

THE USE OF ANIMAL SKINS TO MAKE garments goes back to Paleolithic times, but untreated, the raw hides soon became stiff and perished. It was not until Neolithic times that the basic process of vegetable tanning is thought to have been discovered. Vegetable tanning involves soaking animal skins in tannic acid – a solution made from tree bark (particularly oak), galls, roots, and fruits – which makes the leather pliable and able to last for years.

Today, sophisticated cutting, sewing, and shaping techniques are used to make everything from shoes and jackets to bridles and saddles. Handling and sewing leather for more complicated items involves a high degree of skill. Saddlers are often apprenticed for up to seven years in order to perfect their craft. At the less utilitarian end of the scale highly

sophisticated decorating techniques have been developed. Recent years have seen the flowering of a new group of professional designer-leatherworkers. Through exhibitions, conferences, and training they seek to push the boundaries of this craft further and further and to gain wider recognition for the twentieth-century craftsmakers working with this versatile and durable material.

Leather does not necessarily need to be elaborately tooled and decorated. Careful choice of materials and finishes plays an enormous role in the quality of the finished article. The techniques explained here can, with experience, be adapted to make a container for any musical instrument – from a flute to a French horn – but for larger objects specialist skills in woodwork as well as leatherwork are necessary.

Traditional leatherworking skills and a number of specialist tools and materials are necessary to achieve good results. Care should be taken to choose vegetable-tanned leather, not modern chrome- or currier-prepared leather. The leather is molded to the instrument itself, and the stitching, the close-fitting lid, and the combination of color and texture work together to give a sense of wholeness to the finished design.

To make the whistle case, the following materials are needed: a replica of a whistle, called a former, made from a length of wooden doweling (see page 192), a piece of ⅛ in (4 mm) thick vegetable-tanned oxhide (cowhide), contact adhesive, hand-hot water in a large bowl, heavy natural linen thread, a small block of beeswax, fine-grade sandpaper, aniline dye, shellac, denatured

A STURDY QUALITY
*Brass locks and fittings add strength as well
as decorative detail to a case.*

alcohol, and natural leather polish.

Also gather together the following pieces of equipment: a cutting board, a craft knife, a metal straight-edge, a medium-sized hammer, saddler's clams, dividers or a leather pricking iron with six stitches per 1 in (2.5 cm), a sharp diamond-bladed awl, a medium edge shave, two harness needles, a cork block, a medium-height stool, and a small piece of sheepskin.

The finished case is made wholly of leather. It requires no integral wooden structure and thus needs a solid former to go inside it while it is being made. Using the whistle as a model, shape the

A CASE FOR A FLUTE
*This unusually shaped flute case has been
molded on a specially-made wooden former.*

SMOOTH, SCULPTED LINES
*Great skill is required in molding and
shaping the leather for a violin case.*

top of the former by whittling the dowel and adding masking tape in several thicknesses to make the shape of the mouthpiece of the whistle. It is very important to spend time getting this part right, as it affects the quality of the finished instrument case; the result should present a very even profile. Polish the former to make it slippery and to prevent the glue from sticking to it.

Measure the circumference of the former, allowing ⅜ in (1 cm) excess. Using the craft knife and metal straightedge on the cutting board, cut a strip of leather to this width for the case. Make it the same length as the former to allow for shrinkage of the leather during molding and stitching.

Using contact adhesive, glue along the edge of the leather at the bottom and sides. Fold the strip in half, so that you

have a long tube, and hammer down until the glue has taken and the joining is firm. As the former is not yet in the case, take care not to squash the edge.

Immerse the case in hand-hot water until the leather is thoroughly soaked and pliable. This should take about one minute. Make sure that you keep the leather clean and avoid contact with steel or iron once the leather is wet – it will blemish it. Now ease the wet leather over the former until it is completely home. Using the nails on your thumb and forefinger, score a line for the stitching to follow along the bottom and side.

Pull the case off the former, then, using the dividers or pricking iron, mark the stitching holes along the nail-marked line, leaving ⅛ in (4 mm) between stitches, or, six or seven stitches per 1 in (2.5 cm).

Using the sharp, diamond-bladed awl, make stitching holes where marked by pressing the awl through the leather at an even angle onto the cork block. Stop within 1¼ in (3.2 cm) of the top of the case. Measure a thread four times longer than the seam. Wax the thread by pulling it over the block of beeswax. Apply more wax to the ends to make threading the needles easier.

For saddle stitching you will require a needle on both ends of the thread. To thread one needle, pierce the thread with the needle about 2½ in (6.5 cm) in from the end. Pass the short tail through the eye of the needle, and pull the thread back over it until it is tight, leaving a tail the same length as the needle. Thread the other end in the same way.

Sitting on the stool, take the saddler's clams between your knees at a comfort-

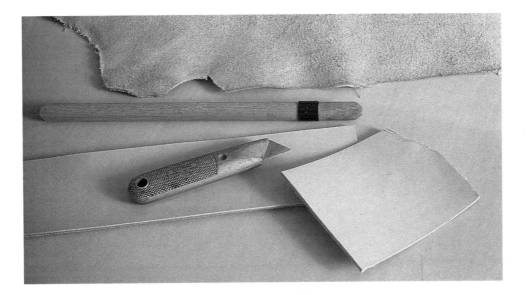

THE FORMER
A replica of the whistle is made out of doweling and masking tape. The leather is molded around the former to make sure that the whistle will fit the case exactly.

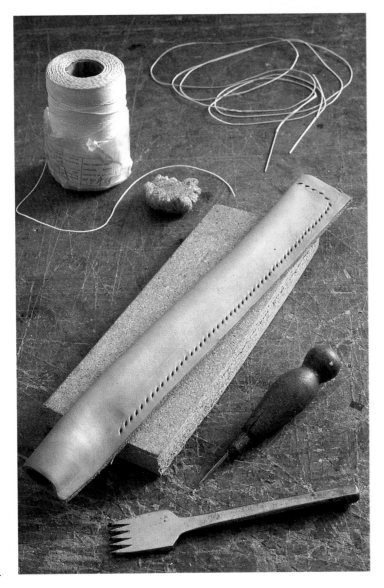

STITCHING THE CASE
The case is held firmly between the knees with saddler's clams while stitching (above).

PUNCHING HOLES IN THE LEATHER
With a cork block as a base, a pricking iron is used to create evenly spaced holes.

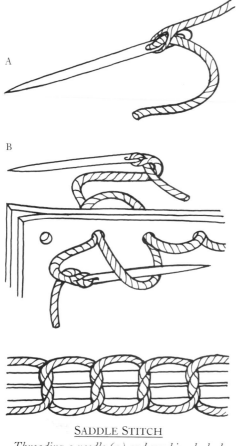

SADDLE STITCH
Threading a needle (a) and working locked saddle stitch (b).

TRIMMING AND FINISHING
Excess leather is cut away very close to the stitching for a good finish.

able height. Place the leather case in the clams and, starting at the base, put one needle through the first hole. Pull the thread until there is the same length of thread on each side of the hole. Put the left-hand needle through the second hole and pull it through. Pick up the needle with your right hand so that both are held in the same hand. Thread the other needle through the second hole, pulling the thread at the same time with the left hand. To "lock" the stitches, put the needle through the last loop and pull both threads firmly together, toward you. The aim is to achieve an even saddle stitch, going the same way all the time. Saddle stitch to the last 1¼ in (3.2 cm) leaving the ends trailing.

In order for the cap to fit snugly over the top of the case, the leather must now be cut to lie flat. Place the former back in

the case, and pull the unstitched, top edge apart. Lap the leather flat over itself and cut through both thicknesses onto the former. Trim away the excess so that the leather butts together. Then trim the end of the case so that it is ¾ in (2 cm) shorter than the former. Leave the case in a warm place to dry.

When the case is dry, mark the stitching holes in the last 1¼ in (3.2 cm) of the seam with the pricking iron. Keep the case on the the former, marking both sides of the butt joint about ⅛ in (4 mm) in from each side of the joining. When making the holes, use the awl at a 30 degree angle down to the former from each side, coming out within the thickness of the leather, not pressing right through. Re-thread the needles and stitch across the butt so that the seam lies flat. Finish off by reversing the last few

stitches and trimming the ends.

To make the cap, use exactly the same techniques, molding the leather over the end of the former and leather case. Place plastic wrap around the leather case to protect it. Trim the leather away very close to the stitching and leave it to dry. Form a bevel edge on the cap with the edge shave, and sandpaper it smooth while it is still dry. Then re-dampen the case and cap so that the dye will take more smoothly. Dip the piece of sheepskin in the aniline dye, and smooth the dye over the whole of the outside of the case and the cap. Wipe the leather with an old cloth while it is still wet, and then leave it to dry. When it is dry, seal the leather with a little shellac (thinned if necessary with the alcohol). When this has dried, polish the whistle case until a rich shine is achieved.

SPONGE-WARE

<u>SHELVES OF DECORATIVE DISHES</u>
A combination of sponging and stenciling techniques have been used to decorate these plates, bowls, and jugs.

Pots are among the earliest artifacts archeologists have discovered, and the versatility of clay has ensured that no civilization has ever abandoned the craft. As a result, there are countless different methods for making and decorating pots, and in many of them mechanization and handwork have developed side by side.

Josiah Wedgwood pioneered the mass production of ceramics in England in the mid-eighteenth century and did so by dividing all the various stages of production among the workers. Some processes were later taken over by machines, but even in the largest factories pots are still thrown and sometimes decorated by hand.

The two most usual ways of shaping clay by hand are throwing and building. Throwing is done on a potter's wheel,

PLASTER MOLDS
*Clay is laid over the outside surface of the
mold, and pressed gently to fit.*

TRIMMING THE EDGE
*A cheese wire is used to cut excess clay away
from the profile of the mold.*

which is turned while the potter shapes a
form from a ball of clay. Pot-throwing
looks simple but in fact requires considerable skill. Built pots are easier to
make; they can be made from slabs of
raw clay or from coiled strips.

Surface pattern can be added in the
form of painted decoration. Spongeware
decoration is one of the simplest and
most rewarding types of ceramic painting. Natural sponges are used to apply
the color, and each sponge has a unique
texture. The designs can thus be successfully repeated, giving just that degree of
variety within similarity that character-
izes hand decoration. A combination of

GLAZING THE PLATE
*After biscuit firing, the plate is dipped into
white glaze and allowed to dry overnight.*

SPONGE DECORATING
*The surface of the plate is sponged all over
using a weak cobalt oxide solution.*

stenciled motifs, sponging, and free-hand painting creates a rhythmic pattern of sharp and soft outlines.

To make a sponged or stenciled plate, similar to the ones shown, the slab method is used. The following materials are required: a bag of red earthenware clay; 2 lb (1 kg) opaque tin glaze (which should be bought from the same supplier as the clay to ensure its exact compatibility); 4 oz (100 g) blue cobalt oxide; 4 oz (100 g) yellow and black glaze stains, if the plate is to be stenciled; and liquid wax.

The equipment needed consists of: two wooden battens 1 x ⅜ x 18 in (2.5 x 1 x 46 cm); several good-sized pieces of burlap or cambric; an ordinary rolling pin; a plaster-of-Paris plate mold (obtainable from pottery suppliers) or a wooden plate frame (see page 200); a

wire cheese cutter; a potter's "kidney" made of rubber or plastic for smoothing the clay; a sheet of polyethylene; a small cosmetic sponge; glass jars for mixing the glazes; fine paintbrushes; stencil paper; a small natural sponge; a fine-mesh glaze sieve; and an electric kiln with an automatic cut-off switch (schools that run pottery classes often have a kiln available for use by members of the public). A decorating wheel may also be useful.

From the main mass of clay, cut a block weighing approximately 2 lb (1 kg), depending on the size of the mold to be covered. Next "wedge" the clay. This involves cutting and pummeling the clay on a firm surface to remove any trapped air bubbles. Place the wedged clay on a piece of burlap and roll it out evenly by turning the clay over and

through 90 degrees every couple of passes with the rolling pin. When it is nearly the right thickness, approximately ⅜ in (1 cm), place the battens each side of the clay and roll the rolling pin along them – keep rolling until the clay is level with the battens. The slab of clay should be slightly larger than the mold. Even out any surface imperfections with the kidney, dipped in water.

Lift the rolled-out clay by resting it over the rolling pin and then lay it over the mold. Gently press the clay to fit the contours of the mold exactly. Finally, smooth the surface with the kidney. Use the cheese wire to cut excess clay away from the edge of the mold. Smooth the edges with a damp cosmetic sponge.

Cover the clay with a sheet of polyethylene and leave it in a cool place to dry; this takes about 24 hours. The drying

APPLYING STENCILS
*Flower motifs are cut out of heavy stencil
paper and laid on a plate.*

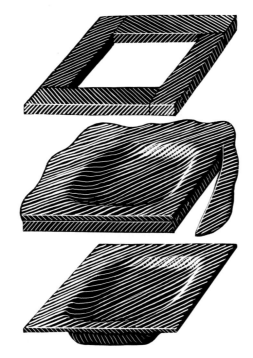

PAINTING THE FLOWERS
*When the cobalt oxide is dry, the details are
painted freehand.*

A WOODEN PLATE FRAME

To make a square-plate frame, four 2 x 1 in (5 x 2.5 cm) battens, each at least 8 in (20 cm) long are required. Nail these together so that the outside of the frame measures 12 in (30 cm) square and 1 in (2.5 cm) deep.

Roll out the clay as directed. Place the frame on a piece of cloth and lay the sheet of clay over it. Press the clay gently into the bottom and up the sides, easing it into the corners. Using the cheese wire, trim the edges level with the outside edge of the frame. Smooth with the kidney and damp sponge.

Leave the plate to dry for 24 hours. Turn it out gently onto the cloth and leave for another two to four days, turning regularly. The plate can then be fired and decorated in the same way as a plate prepared on a plaster mold.

process should not be hurried or carried out in a warm room; otherwise the clay will crack. When it is dry, the clay will have shrunk noticeably and be leather hard. To remove the plate from the mold, place a flat board against the bottom of the plate and, in one swift movement, turn the board and plate over so that the plate is resting on the board. Lift the mold out.

Leave the plate to dry for another two to four days. Turn it over every eight hours or so to prevent warping.

When the clay is dry, it can be placed in the kiln for biscuit firing. Switch on the kiln to a low setting. After two to four hours – depending on the size of the kiln and the number of pieces in it – the temperature will reach between 390–750°F (200–400°C). The temperature should rise no more than 212°F (100°C)

<u>HARD-WEARING DESIGNS</u>
*Dishes look good as a display but they are
highly functional, too.*

in any one hour. Then turn the kiln up to a medium setting for three to four hours until it reaches approximately 1200–1300°F (650–700°C). Finally, turn the kiln up to a high setting, 1830°F (1000°C), until it switches itself off automatically. Leave the plate to cool slowly in the kiln.

Remove the plate from the kiln, and paint the base with liquid wax. Make the tin glaze according to the manufacturer's instructions, and pour it through a fine sieve several times into a dish washing bowl. Holding the plate lightly at the edges, dip it into the glaze for several seconds to coat it evenly all over (the wax on the base will resist the glaze). Lift it out and allow the excess glaze to run off the plate. Leave the plate to dry overnight. Any unevenness can be rubbed out with your fingers and

small uncoated areas can be touched in. If any glaze has attached to the base, remove it with a damp sponge.

To decorate the plate, place it on a decorating wheel or a raised surface. The plate can be sponged, stenciled, or decorated with a combination of the two. Sponges always have one fine and one coarse side, so it is possible to choose the texture that will make the most pleasing pattern. A sponged effect is achieved by dipping a natural sponge into weak cobalt oxide (one teaspoon of cobalt oxide to one and a half teacups of water). Make sure the sponge is saturated. Squeeze out any excess cobalt oxide and gently dab the sponge onto the surface of the plate. Repeat this process until the entire surface of the plate has been covered with a sponge pattern.

To decorate the plate with stencil

motifs, cut flower shapes out of stencil paper. Mix the cobalt oxide in the same way as for sponging. Mix up the yellow and black glaze stains (half a teaspoon of stain to half a teacup of water). Position the stencils on the plate, and sponge or paint cobalt over the surface. Carefully lift off the stencils. When the cobalt oxide has dried, paint the yellow centers of the flowers and the black lines on the petals freehand.

The decoration should be left to dry for about eight hours before the plate is glaze fired. The kiln should be on a medium setting for two hours. Bring the temperature up to about 1830°F (1000°C) – check the glaze supplier's instructions for exact specifications – at a rate of 212°F (100°C) every hour, then leave it to cool thoroughly and remove from the kiln.

STENCILED TILES

SURFACE DECORATION
*Stenciled motifs are only one form of
decoration. The tiles drying (right) are
destined for marbling.*

TILES CAN BE FOUND IN ALMOST every architectural context worldwide. Among the most charming for interior use are the blue and white, tin-glazed, Dutch Delftware tiles, made from the sixteenth century onward. The freely painted scenes of everyday life found on Delftware were popular throughout the whole of Northern Europe, America, and England. Gradually Dutch potters began to settle and manufacture their wares in England. English and Dutch tiles from the early eighteenth century are extremely difficult to tell apart, but by about 1750 distinctive styles and technical differences had emerged. One hundred years later, tiles were being mass-produced by every method the ceramic industry could devise, but hand-decorating skills were never lost,

and tin-glazed tiles are regaining popularity once again.

The contemporary ceramic artist making decorative tiles has a range of techniques to choose from: working on pre-fired blanks and painting, spraying, sponging, or stenciling colored designs by hand; applying printed ceramic transfers; or creating the design in high or low relief by various methods.

Relief tiles are made by pressing wet clay into shaped plaster molds, or by modeling forms freely in soft clay and joining them to a flat, wet clay blank. These sculptural surfaces may be highly colored and glazed, like tiles found in the Mediterranean or Islamic countries, or can be of simple terracotta (unglazed red earthenware). Modeled terracotta was frequently used, from the Renaissance to the nineteenth century, for

panels of architectural decoration, as friezes and moldings or in fireplaces and door frames. Terracotta can be worked in high or low relief; it can be smooth, textured, or burnished to a dull sheen.

Modern studio ceramists will often combine several techniques in a single tile project. For instance, a tile panel could have a painted figurative scene with a molded patterned border, incorporating the same colors. Such panels are frequently commissioned for specific domestic situations, such as kitchens, fireplaces, hallways, friezes, or floor areas, and also for public places.

In a small commercial workshop the process for making flat, decorative tiles – from the commissioning of the design to the laying of the tiles – can take from six to eight weeks. Flat, blank tiles are first prepared in batches of ten or more.

PLAIN GLAZED TILES
Flat tiles, coated with white tin glaze must be thoroughly dry before decorating.

APPLYING THE STENCIL
To ensure that the pattern aligns, the stencil must be carefully positioned on the tile.

MAKING A STENCIL
Cut out stencils with a sharp x-acto to give a clearly defined motif.

The clay – red earthenware in this case – is wedged to remove all the air bubbles and then cut into thick slices and thumped or thrown into plaster-of-Paris molds. The surface of the mold is scraped over with a long knife blade to level the top of the clay, and the wet tile is then tipped out onto a board to dry.

The tiles are laid out, sixty to a board, and left to dry at an even, moderate temperature for approximately two weeks. They are then biscuit-fired in an electric kiln. When the tiles have cooled down, they are ready to glaze. The front surface of the tiles is skimmed over a deep tray of white tin glaze. This dries to a soft powdery finish, onto which colored oxides can be applied. Designs are stenciled, painted freehand, spattered, or sponged onto the glazed tile. A ceramist decorates 20 or more tiles at once, work-

ing along a line. The stencil is positioned on the blank tile, weighted at the corners and dabbed through with color. The motifs can be applied to the glaze in solid or textured areas which dry almost immediately, allowing one stencil to follow the last in quick succession. When decorated, the tiles are loaded into cranks, placed in an electric kiln, and fired for eight hours. The kiln is cooled overnight and emptied the next day. Colors and quality are checked and matched to existing fired tiles; completing a scheme might take three or four more firings.

The amateur wishing to make decorative tiles without the back-up of a workshop should use blank ready-made ceramic tiles. Decoration is applied in the same way, using enamel colors in tubes (available from pottery suppliers),

TIME AND AGAIN
Stencils can be used more than once to repeat the same pattern.

IN PROPORTION
Plan a stencil design to fill the area of the tile without looking crowded or busy.

instead of colored oxides.

Stenciled decoration combines the possibilities of easy repetition of a motif with freedom of color choice and surface. Up to eight colors can be used, applied with small natural sponges or a paintbrush. Several stencils can be used for each tile.

To make a stencil, first work out a design that suits the proportions of the tile, filling the area well. Draw it on flimsy paper, then lay it over a sheet of carbon paper, facing onto heavy stencil paper. Go over the lines again to transfer it to the stencil paper. Each stencil can be used for one or two colors, though these can be varied at will. Make the stencil ⅜ in (1 cm) larger, all around, than the tile, to make it easier to handle. Nick a corner of the stencil paper to help ensure that it aligns with the tile and the stencils

for the other colors correctly. Cut the stencil using a sharp x-acto knife on a firm cutting board, making sure that the cut-out areas are not too close together.

Hold the stencil carefully in position, load a sponge or paintbrush with color and dab through the holes in the stencil. When the enamel is dry, add the next color and so on until the tiles are complete. The tiles can then be fired by the amateur in a small enameling kiln to a temperature of 1352°F (750°C). The firing will make the enamel design relatively permanent, resisting all except sharp scratches.

THREE-TIER DESIGN
The fruit bowl design is made up of three separate stencils — you can use more than one color in each layer.

STAINED GLASS

<u>COLOR AND LIGHT</u>
*Stained glass has a warmth and vitality that
can only be fully realized when it is
illuminated by natural light.*

STAINED GLASS IS ONE OF THE OLD-est architectural crafts and one of the few that have never been mechanized. It probably has its origins in Germany; the earliest stained glass windows to have survived are in Augsburg Cathedral and date from 1605. Medieval craftsmen were often itinerant, and as the glaziers traveled across Europe, the art of stained glass spread gradually through France, England, and the Low Countries. It may seem surprising at first that it should have been there, in the darker countries of northern Europe, that stained glass developed; but the muted, changing light was found to bring out the subtleties of colored windows, making "fine weather in church," as Proust described it, all year round.

During the Reformation in the six-teenth century many stained glass win-dows were destroyed, and the craft then went into a decline which lasted until the nineteenth century. When it was re-vived it was used in both religious and domestic contexts, and today it continues to be practiced in a variety of ways.

The term "stained" glass refers to the process used to obtain yellow, by stain-ing clear glass with silver nitrate. Other colors are obtained in different ways. They can be applied to the surface with enamel paint for transparent colors, or iron oxides for opaque colors. Glass — either hand-blown or machine-rolled — can also be bought ready colored. Another type of glass that is commonly used is "flashed glass." This is basically clear with a thin surface layer of color, through which a pattern can be cut.

Traditionally all stained glass in-cluded painted or etched details. Many modern craftsmen, however, use only plain-colored glass. Today it is possible to make much larger single sheets than were feasible in the past. This, along with the use of concrete instead of lead to support the structure, has made it easy to achieve large-scale effects with stained glass that would have been impossible for the medieval glazier.

Stained glass panels such as the ones shown here can be hung in front of a window or inserted as a single pane, provided the window frame is deep enough. Painting, etching, and staining techniques have been used to add surface interest. For those unfamiliar with glass decoration, it is advisable to attempt only the painting technique.

Much of the equipment for making stained glass can be found in an art shop. The glass itself can be bought in any

DECORATIVE PANELS
*Modern designs can be used in many
architectural contexts.*

WORKING WITH GLASS
*An illuminated work surface is used to assess
color and pattern.*

quantity, and scraps for experiments are usually available cheaply. For the panel shown on page 211, three kinds of glass are used: machine-rolled, ready-colored glass for the bottom section; plain window glass for the middle area; and flashed glass for the top section. Iron oxide, fine oil such as lavender oil, gum arabic, blue enamel paint and silver nitrate are required for coloring and decorating the glass.

Other essentials are a glass cutter with a steel wheel, glass pliers, paintbrushes, a palette knife, a soldering iron with a copper bit, dry plaster, flux (such as tallow), and lead. This is bought in strips of either "H" section, for joining glass, or "U" section for edges (required only if the panel will hang free). This should be cut with a lead knife. The glass is held in place with a stiff paste made from

equal parts of plaster of Paris and whiting, mixed with equal parts of linseed oil and mineral spirit. Black powder-paint should be used to darken it. Flat-sided nails, a lightweight hammer, an oyster knife, a wooden board, two battens, and some steel wool are needed for the leading-up stage. For firing the glass a small enameling kiln is required.

The panel illustrated on page 211 measures 6¾ x 9½ in (17 x 24 cm). The starting point is a colored sketch the same size as the finished panel, with black lines drawn accurately to the actual width of the leads. If a different design is used, it should not include any pieces of glass less than 1 in (2.5 cm) square or any angles exceeding 180 degrees. A rectangular format less than 2 ft (60 cm) square is recommended.

Make an accurate tracing of your

sketch and use this as a template to cut out each of the glass sections.

Paint the design free-hand on the underside of the bottom section with iron oxide. This comes in powder form and should be mixed with water, using a palette knife, on a flat surface. Add a drop of the fine oil, and a little gum arabic, which helps the iron oxide to stick to the glass.

In the middle section the design is etched and then colored. Etching should only be attempted with professional supervision under well-ventilated, studio conditions. For the etching, both sides of the glass are covered with adhesive-backed vinyl, then, on one side, a pattern is cut away with a craft knife. The glass is immersed in a tray of hydrofluoric acid for any time between five minutes and one hour, depending on the

TRELLIS OF BIRDS
This unusual chapel window (right) has been
etched, enameled, and painted.

SOOTHING BLUES
The mottled transparency of blue enamel
creates a sense of tranquility.

depth of etching required. When the glass is removed from the acid the vinyl is peeled away to reveal the pattern.

Color is added to the top surface of the middle section by brushing blue enamel paint over it and then cleaning the color away from the etched areas of the pattern. It is important that this is done on the top surface; otherwise the back of the glass will stick to the bottom of the kiln when it is fired. Next, paint silver nitrate onto the back of the glass over the area intended to be yellow. Then brush iron oxide onto the top surface to create the dark lines on the motifs.

The bird shape can be etched into the colored surface of the top section using the process already described. Decorate this section by painting the surface with iron oxide as required.

All three sections must now be fired.

THE PANEL DESIGN
*Once a sketch has been made, the glass can be
cut, and pattern and color introduced.*

The kiln shelf should be covered with a bed of dry plaster to prevent the glass from sticking. Lay the pieces of glass on the shelf, and raise the kiln temperature to 1185°F (640°C). Once that heat is reached, switch off the kiln and leave it to cool (about twelve hours). The color is now permanently fixed.

For leading-up, pin the template to the board, and nail two battens over it at right angles along the right-hand and bottom edges. Place the strips of lead that will form the bottom right-hand corner along the inner edges of the battens. These leads should be "H" section if the panel is to be used in a window, or "U" section if it is to be hung separately.

Assemble the pieces, working outward from the bottom right-hand corner. Hold each section of glass in place with flat-sided nails while the next

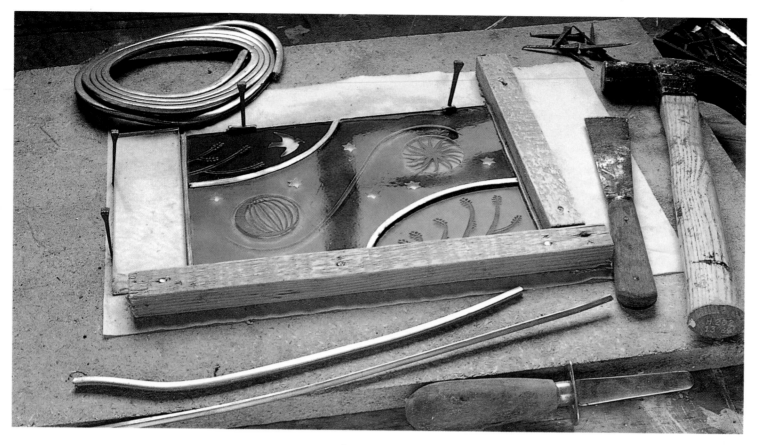

LEADING-UP
*Battens hold the glass in place. The leads
have been blackened in the finished panel.*

length of lead is cut. Leads that join two pieces of glass should all be "H" section. An oyster knife can be used to ease the glass into them. A spare piece of glass or a ruler can be fixed down the left-hand side of the frame as the work progresses, to keep it square.

When all the pieces are assembled, clean the lead joints with steel wool. Rub tallow onto them and solder them. The panel is now loosely held together and should be turned over carefully and soldered on the other side. Mix the plaster of Paris paste and rub it into all the joints on both sides. Dust the panel with more plaster of Paris. Any surplus paste between the glass and the leads can be removed with a stick, and finally brushed off. As a finishing touch, to make the leads a matte black, paint them with a layer of grate polish.

JEWELRY

<u>AN INDIVIDUAL PERSONALITY</u>
*Jewelers develop their own particular style,
the gold and silver brooch above is an
essentially spontaneous creation.*

SINCE TIME BEGAN, PEOPLE HAVE adorned themselves with jewelry — whether for purely aesthetic purposes or for more symbolic, ceremonial, or religious reasons. The extraordinary variety of materials and techniques used to make jewelry — some new, some ancient — are a continual source of fascination and inspiration.

Traditionally, jewelry has both reflected the character of the wearer and indicated his or her status. Since the 1960s, however, some jewelers, particularly in Holland, Britain, Germany, and North America, have challenged accepted ideas about the design, scale, and function of jewelry. Cheap materials, such as paper, plastics, and tin, have been used in outsize forms which redefine rather than simply complement the body. This "new jewelry" move-

ment has enlivened the craft of jewelry and revealed affinities with performance art and fashion design. Even so, it has not diminished the popular delight in the more traditional jewelry designs.

The work shown is made of semiprecious stones, gold, and silver. Although the pieces are contemporary, the simplicity of the techniques and the spontaneous working of traditional raw materials echo closely the jewelry of Africa and ancient Egypt.

The necklaces are composed of beads shaped individually from semiprecious gemstones. Lapis lazuli, cornelian, garnet, and amethyst are among the stones used, and the final character of each bead is determined by the way it is cut on a diamond wheel and shaped on a grinder, and by the length of time it spends in a tumbler (a rotating cylindrical box con-

taining abrasive powder) which refines its shape and gives it polish. Lapidary shops can provide an all-in-one machine which contains the cutting, grinding, and tumbling units. The beads are strung on polyester thread, made by the rope-making technique.

A brooch is a good first project, since it is made using simple equipment and techniques. The materials and equipment needed are: a sheet of $1/64$ in (0.4 mm) thick silver, or cheaper metal, such as copper, approximately 4 x 6 in (10 x 15 cm); flux; medium silver solder; a dilute solution of sulfuric acid (25 parts water to 1 part sulfuric acid, ask your druggist to mix this), or pickling solution (obtainable from specialist suppliers); a reel of $1/32$ in (0.8 mm) diameter stainless steel dental wire (from dental suppliers); 1 in (2.5 cm) of

<u>PLANNING A NECKLACE</u>
*The jeweler carefully coordinates stones on a
sheet of corrugated cardboard.*

<u>SEMIPRECIOUS STONES</u>
*The gemstones are individually shaped and
smoothed – giving them a rough charm.*

narrow silver tube; a sheet of very fine
emery paper; straight shears; a hammer
and anvil (or a flat metal surface); a soldering torch; a needle file; a small pair of
pliers; an 8 in (20 cm) engineer's file,
and some pattern-making tools.

Using the shears, cut the brooch out
of the metal sheet so that it measures 2 x
1½ in (5 x 4 cm). Then cut a long strip
off the sheet. Cut this into four narrower
strips, which should each be a little
longer than the sides of the brooch.
These strips will form the frame around
the "picture" of the brooch. Hammer
each strip on the anvil, shaping them
carefully so that they are reasonably

<u>BROOCH DESIGNS</u>
*Using the same basic techniques a wide range
of designs can be achieved.*

216

A COLLECTION OF NECKLACES
*The necklaces look deceptively simple with
their sympathetic arrangement of beads.*

straight and ready for soldering. Before soldering, brush flux evenly onto the surface of the brooch and the strips.

Soldering fuses the strips to the brooch. To do this, lay the strips down at right angles to each other on the brooch edge, with the end of each strip jutting out slightly beyond the edge of the brooch. Cut the medium silver solder into about nine specks, and place them around the edges of the brooch.

Soldering is something that needs a little practice, but think of the solder as a glue that melts only when hot. The soldering temperature for silver solder is just under 1472°F (800°C). With one

EAR PIECES
*Earrings display many of the features of the
jeweler's work*

TRIMMING AND SHAPING
*When the frame is securely attached, the edges
can be trimmed and filed (below).*

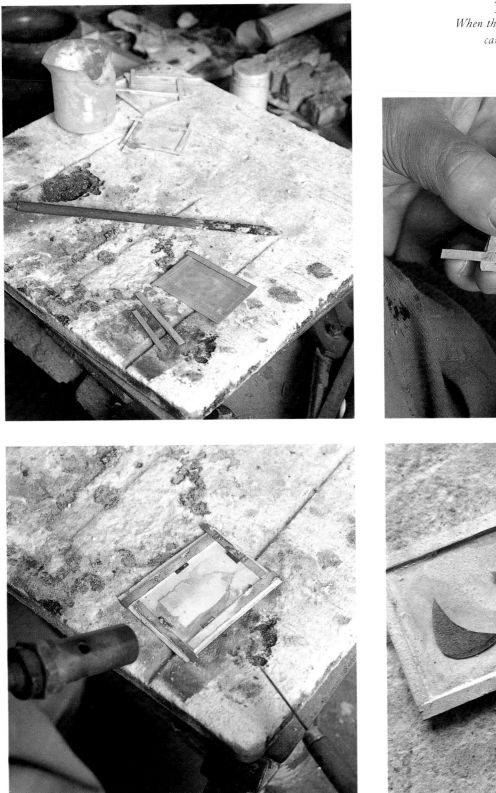

FRAMING THE BROOCH
*Strips of silver are soldered firmly around the
edge of the rectangle (above).*

ADDING DECORATION
*Offcuts of silver and gold are introduced to
embellish the design.*

NEARING COMPLETION
After soldering the brooch is cleaned and additional decoration can be added.

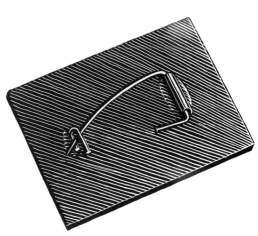

BACK MATTERS
A short length of silver tube and a piece of dental wire make a sturdy fastening.

hand, play the soldering torch evenly over the surface of the strips. Holding a needle file in your other hand, use it to push the solder under the edges of the strips, so that the strips and brooch fuse. The solder should run freely into the hottest parts of the work. Try not to get solder onto the body of the strips, as it will show. If there is a gap in the frame strips, fill it with solder.

Pick the brooch up with the small pliers, or anything else that will withstand the heat, and plunge it into cold water. Dry it, and then hammer the brooch frame down all the way around on the anvil. Then reheat the joining just to make sure that the brooch is well soldered. If any areas are not stuck firm, repeat the soldering process.

Trim the edges of the brooch, using the shears, then file them with the engineer's file. Clean the brooch in the dilute sulfuric acid solution or the pickling solution for about two hours.

Decoration can be punched directly onto the brooch, creating all sorts of patterns or a picture, using tools such as ground-down files, nails, punches with different ends, and so on. Alternatively, shapes can be cut out from silver sheet and applied. Solder the shapes to the brooch in the same way as the framing strips. This brooch has a silver moon, incised stars and a gold sun. Brass can be used instead of gold, although brass does tarnish. If you are making a brass and copper brooch, use brazing rod (available from a specialist supplier) instead of silver solder.

The fastening of the brooch is made using a length of dental wire, held by a silver tube and fastened to a hook at the other end. Take the silver tube and solder it to the back of the brooch. Then take the dental wire and bend over a small section of the end. Hold the wire against the side of the tube and draw the wire across the brooch to judge how long the fastening needs to be. Cut the wire and file the end to a point. To make the hook, solder one end of a long piece of wire onto the brooch (to avoid burning yourself). When cool, cut it down to less than $\frac{1}{2}$ in (1.2 cm) and bend it into a hook. Pass the cut fastening wire through the tube at one end securing it with the bent end. There should be tension in the wire when it is finally slipped under the hook.

When this is completed, clean the brooch in the acid or pickling solution and rub it down with very fine emery paper. Polish the brooch to finish.

INDEX

Page numbers in *italic* refer to the illustrations

air-drying, flowers, 150
animal toys, *187*
apples: cider making, 141-3, *141-3*
  herb-apple jelly, 135
appliqué, 26, 33-6, *33-6*
Armenian bole, 173-4, *173*, 175
Art and Crafts Movement, 38

basketry, 145-8, *145-8*
beeswax candles, 158, *160, 161*
Bewick, Thomas, 89
binding, books, 98-101, *98-101*, 170
birds, carved, 177-81, *177-81*
Blake, William, 89
blanket stitch, *35*
bloaters, *127*
block printing, fabrics, 15-19, *15-19*
blow torches, 180-1, *180*
bole, Armenian, 173-4, *173*, 175
bookmarks, ikat weaving, *62*, 64-5, *65*
books: bookbinding, 98-101, *98-101*, 170

letterpress printing, 92-4
  marbled endpapers, 78
braids, 54, *56, 57*
brass, jewelry, 219
bread, festival, 117-21, *117-21*
brooches, 214-19, *215, 218-19*
brushes, for papermarbling, 80-1, *80*
buttons, *53*

cable stitch, smocking, 42
calligraphy, *84-7*, 85-7, 170
candies, chocolate making, *128-31*, 129-31
candle making, 158-61, *158-61*
carving: birds, 177-81, *177-81*
  stick dressing, *164-7*, 165-7
ceramics: spongeware, 196-201, *196-201*
  stenciled tiles, 202-5, *202-5*
cheese, goat, 110-14, *110-15*
chintz, 15
chocolate making, *128-31*, 129-31
Christianity, 117-18, 122
Christmas, 122
cider making, 141-3, *141-3*
clay: ceramics, 196-201, *196-201*
  tiles, 204
clowns, toy, *189*

cocoa beans, 129
Columella, 132
combs, for papermarbling, 81, *81*
cookie: chocolate making, *128-31*, 129-31
  cookie making, 122-3, *122-3*
  festival bread, 117-21, *117-21*
  goat cheese, 110-14, *110-15*
  preserves, 132-9, *132-9*
  smoking fish, 125-7, *125-7*
  cookie making, 122-3, *122-3*
cooling mats, basketry, 145-8, *145, 149*
copper, jewelry, 219
cording, pillows, 24
crooks, stick dressing, 165
Culpeper, Nicholas, 150
curds, 132, *132*, 138-9, *138-9*
cutters, cookie, *122*, 123

decoys, 177
Delftware, 202
desiccants, dried flowers, 150
dipped candles, 158, *159*, 160-1
discharge dyeing, 15
distressing, gilding, *175*, 175
dockers, festival bread, *119*, 120
dolls, papier mâché, *104-6*, 105-6
dried flowers, 150-5, *150-5*

cocoa beans, 129
driftwood, carved birds, 177, *177*, 178
drinks, cider making, 141-3, *141-3*
dyeing: hand block printing, 15-19, *15-19*
  ikat weaving, 61-5, *61-5*
  yarn, 45-50, *45-51*

ear-rings, *217*
Easter cookies, 122, 123, *123*
embroidery, smocking, 38-42, *38-43*
engraving, wood, *88-91*, 89-91
etching, stained glass, 208-9, *209*

fabrics *see* textiles
Fair Isle knitting, 50
feather quills, *84*
festival bread, 117-21, *117-21*
fish, smoking, 125-7, *125-7*
fitching, basketry, *148*, 149
'flashed glass', 207
flowers: dried, 150-5, *150-5*
  dyes, 45
fondant cream chocolates, 131
food *see* cookery
frames: gilding, 170-5, *170-5*
  quilting, 22, 23, *23*

tassels, 56, *56*
French knots, *35*
fruit, preserves, 132-9, *132-9*

gemstones, jewelry, 214, *215*
gesso: calligraphy, 85-7
  gilding, *172,* 173
gilding *see* gold
glass, stained, 207-11, *207-11*
glazes, ceramics, *198,* 201
goat cheese, 110-14, *110-15*
gold: calligraphy, 85, 86-7, *87*
  gilding, 170-5, *170-5*
  jewelry, *214, 218,* 219
grapefruit marmalade, 133-4,
  133-4
grasses, dried, 152-3
Gutenberg, Johann, 92

hand block printing, 15-19, *15-19*
harvest loaves, 117-21, *117-21*
herbs: goat cheese, 113, *114*
  herb-apple jelly, 135
herrings, smoked, 126-7, *126,*
  127
honeycomb stitch, smocking, 42
hooked rugs, 66-70, *66-70*
horn, stick dressing, 165-7, *166*
hydrangeas, 153-4, *155*

ikat weaving, 61-5, *61-5*
ink: letterpress printing, 97
  wood engraving, 89

jams, 132-3
jellies, 132-3, *132*
  herb-apple, 135
jewelry, 214-19, *214-19*
Johnston, Edward, 85

kilns: ceramics, 200-1, 204, *205*
  stained glass, 210
knitting, 50-3, *51-3*

lavender, 155
lead, stained glass, 208, 210-11,
  211
leatherwork, *190-5,* 191-5
Legrain, Pierre, 98
lemon curd, 138-9, *138-9*
letterheads, *96,* 97
lettering, calligraphy, *84-7,*
  85-7
letterpress printing, 92-7, *92-7*
linoleum, block printing with,
  16, *18*
Linotype, 92
log cabin patchwork, 26
looms, ikat weaving, 61, *63*

mackerel, smoked, 126
marbling, paper, 78-82, *78-82*
marmalade, 132-3, *133*
metalwork, jewelry, 214-19,
  214-19
milk, goat's, 112, *112*
modeling clay, papier mâché,
  104, 105
Monotype, 92
mordants, 15, 45-6
Morris, William, 15, 98
molds: candles, 158-60, *160*
  papermaking, 76-7, *77*
  pottery, *198,* 199
  relief tiles, 202

necklaces, 214, *215, 217*

oil gilding, 170

paint: papermarbling, 78-82,
  78-82
  on papier mâché, 106
  stained glass, 207, 208, 209
  toys, 187, *188,* 189
paper: bookbinding, 98-100, *100*
  calligraphy, 85, 86
  papermaking, 75-7, *75-7*
  papermarbling, 78-82, *78-82*

papier mâché, 103-6, *103-6*
paraffin wax, candles, 158
parrots, toy, 189, *189*
passementerie, 54-8, *54-9*
patchwork, 26-30, *26-30*
pens, quill, *84,* 85
pickling, 125
picture frames, gilding, 170-5,
  170-5
pictures, appliqué, 33-6, *33-6*
pillows: patchwork, 28, *28-30,*
  29-30
  quilted, 20-4, *21-5*
pirate rocker, 187, 188-9, *188-9*
plants: dried flowers, 150-5,
  150-5
  dyes, 45
plate frames, 200
plates, ceramic, 199-201
Poppies and Pinks jacket, 46,
  50-3, 51-3
'Preening Pintail Mallard', *177,*
  179-81, *180-1*
preserves, 132-9, *132-9*
  smoked fish, 125-7, *125-7*
printing: hand block, 15-19,
  15-19
  letterpress, 92-7, *92-7*
Proust, Marcel, 207

quills, *84*, 85
quilting, 20-4, *20-5*, 34

rag rugs, 66-70, *66-70*
relief printing, 89
religious festivals, 117-18, 122
resist printing, 15
roses, dried, 150, *152*
rugs, rag, 66-70, *66-70*
running stitch, *35*

saddle stitching, 193-5, *194-5*
St Valentine's Day, 122
salmon, smoked, 126, *126*, *127*
salting fish, 125, 126-7
sculpture, papier mâché, 103, *103*
seed stitch, *35*
shawls, hand block printing, 19, *19*
shortbreads, 122
silk, ikat weaving, 61, *62*, 64
silver jewelry, *214*, *218*, 219
smocking, 38-42, *38-43*
smoking fish, 125-7, *125-7*
soldering, 217-19
spongeware, 196-201, *196-201*
stained glass, 207-11, *207-11*
stearin, 158
stenciling: ceramics, 199, *200*,
201
  tiles, 202-5, *202-5*
stick dressing, *164-7*, 165-7
stitches: for appliqué, *35*
  leatherwork, 193-5, *194-5*
  smocking, 41, 42, *43*
stylus, for papermarbling, *81*,
82, *82*
sugar: fondant cream, 131
  preserves, 132, 133

tanning leather, 191
tassels, 54-8, *54-9*
tempering chocolate, 129
templates: festival bread, *118*, 119
  patchwork, 28, *28*, 30
  quilting, 22-3
  toys, 188, *188*
terracotta tiles, 202
textiles: appliqué, 33-6, *33-6*
  dyeing, 45-50, *45-51*
  hand block printing, 15-19,
  15-19
  ikat weaving, 61-5, *61-5*
  knitting, 50-3, *51-3*
  patchwork, 26-30, *26-30*
  quilting, 20-4, *20-5*
  rag rugs, 66-70, *66-70*
  smocking, 38-42, *38-43*

tassels and braids, 54-8, *54-9*
'Three Hens', appliqué, *33-6*,
34-6
throwing pots, 196
tie-dyeing, ikat weaving, 61-5,
63-5
tiles, stenciled, 202-5, *202-5*
toy making, 184-5, *184-5*
trout, smoked, 126
Ts'ai Lun, 75
type, letterpress printing, 94-7,
94-7

vellum: bookbinding, 100
  calligraphy, 86

walking sticks, *164-7*, 165-7
Washington, George, 103
water gilding, 170
wax: candle making, 158-61,
158-61
  wax resist printing, 15
weaving, ikat, 61-5, *61-5*
Wedgwood, Josiah, 196
wheatsheaf loaves, 117-21, *117-21*
whistle cases, leather, 191-5, *191*,
194-5
wicks, candles, 158, 160-1
willow, basketry, 145-8, *145-8*

woad, 47-50
wood: carved birds, 177-81,
177-81
  engraving, *88-91*, 89-91
  plate frames, 200
  stick dressing, *164-7*, 165-7
  toy making, 184-5, *184-5*
writing, calligraphy, 84-7, 85-7

yarn: dyeing, 46-50
  knitting, 50-3, *51-3*

The publisher thanks Jacqui
Hurst for her kind permission to
reproduce the photographs on the
following pages: 38-42, 43
(centre right and bottom right),
44-50, 74-83, 110-15, 122-31,
140-3, 170 and 174 (right). All
other photographs copyright ©
Conran Octopus.

ACKNOWLEDGEMENTS

All the designs in this book are exclusive to the craftspeople featured and must not be reproduced for public exhibition or sale.

The publishers and Martina Margetts would like to express their thanks to the craftspeople:
Julian Akers-Douglas, Janet Bolton, Susan Bosence, Sarah Burnett, Colin Dales, David Constable, Wendy Cushing, Kim Donaldson, David Drew, Jim Edmiston, Amy Emms, Emma Fairfax Lucy, Ann Hechle, John Hinchcliffe and Wendy Barber, Mary Holmes, Mrs Hood, Lucinda Gane, Colin and Pauline Grant, Rosemary Latham, Miriam Macgregor, Caroline Mann, Michael Mitchell, Alison Morton, Breon O'Casey, Marguerite Perry, William and Janet Pinney, Martin Pitt, Mary Restieaux, Mike and Sue Rhodes, Maureen Richardson, Romilly Saumarez Smith, Deborah Schneebeli-Morrell, Jill Spencer, John Stock, Solveig Stone, Guy Taplin, Norman Tulip, Sasha Ward, David Winship and Austin Winstanley.

They would also like to thank the contributors, the Crafts Council of England and Wales, The Handweavers Studio & Gallery, Contemporary Applied Arts, Cirencester Workshops, The Boots Company plc, Gallery Five, Veronica Tongue at Maidstone City Art Gallery, Helen Joseph and Diane Gilder at Shipley Art Gallery, Hilary Paynter and Maureen Briggs.